D1403904

CROCK·POT
·THE ORIGINAL SLOW COOKER·

MEXICAN
SLOW COOKING

pil

Publications International, Ltd.

Copyright © 2017 Publications International, Ltd.

Recipes and text on pages 4–9, 26, 30, 38, 42, 44, 46, 106, 110, 112, 138, 154, 176 and 178 © 2017 Sunbeam Products, Inc. doing business as Jarden Consumer Solutions. All rights reserved. All other recipes and all recipe photographs *except* those on pages 164 and 179 © 2017 Publications International, Ltd.

This publication may not be reproduced or quoted in whole or in part by any means whatsoever without written permission from:

Louis Weber, CEO
Publications International, Ltd.
8140 Lehigh Ave
Morton Grove, IL 60053

Permission is never granted for commercial purposes.

Photographs on front cover and pages 111, 164 and 179 © Shutterstock Images.

Crock-Pot® and the Crock-Pot® logo are registered trademarks of Sunbeam Products, Inc. used under license.

Pictured on the front cover *(clockwise from top):* Pork Tacos with Fresh Salsa *(page 110).*

Pictured on the back cover *(top to bottom, left to right):* Shredded Chicken Tacos *(page 77),* Sweet Potato and Black Bean Chipotle Chili *(page 58),* Black Bean, Zucchini and Corn Enchiladas *(page 125)* and Sweet and Spicy Pork Picadillo *(page 108).*

ISBN: 978-1-64030-122-1

Manufactured in China.

8 7 6 5 4 3 2 1

DISCLAIMER: Food preparation, baking and cooking involve inherent dangers: misuse of electric products, sharp electric tools, boiling water, hot stoves, allergic reactions, foodborne illnesses and the like, pose numerous potential risks. Publications International, Ltd. (PIL) assumes no responsibility or liability for any damages you may experience as a result of following recipes, instructions, tips or advice in this publication.

While we hope this publication helps you find new ways to eat delicious foods, you may not always achieve the results desired due to variations in ingredients, cooking temperatures, typos, errors, omissions, or individual cooking abilities.

CONTENTS

SWEET POTATO AND BLACK BEAN
CHIPOTLE CHILI P. 58

SLOW COOKING TIPS

SIZES OF **CROCK-POT®** SLOW COOKERS

Smaller **CROCK-POT®** slow cookers—such as 1- to 3½-quart models—are the perfect size for cooking for singles, a couple or empty nesters (and also for serving dips).

While medium-size **CROCK-POT®** slow cookers (those holding somewhere between 3 quarts and 5 quarts) will easily cook enough food at one time to feed a small family, they are also convenient for holiday side dishes or appetizers.

Large **CROCK-POT®** slow cookers are great for large family dinners, holiday entertaining and potluck suppers. A 6- to 7-quart model is ideal if you like to make meals in advance. Or, have dinner tonight and store leftovers for later.

TYPES OF **CROCK-POT®** SLOW COOKERS

Current **CROCK-POT®** slow cookers come equipped with many different features and benefits, from auto cook programs to oven-safe stoneware to timed programming. Please visit **WWW.CROCK-POT.COM** to find the **CROCK-POT®** slow cooker that best suits your needs.

How you plan to use a **CROCK-POT®** slow cooker may affect the model you choose to purchase. For everyday cooking, choose a size large enough to serve your family. If you plan to use the **CROCK-POT®** slow cooker primarily for entertaining, choose one of the larger sizes. Basic **CROCK-POT®** slow cookers can hold as little as 16 ounces or as much as 7 quarts. The smallest sizes are great for keeping dips warm on a buffet, while the larger sizes can more readily fit large quantities of food and larger roasts.

COOKING, STIRRING AND FOOD SAFETY

CROCK-POT® slow cookers are safe to leave unattended. The outer heating base may get hot as it cooks, but it should not pose a fire hazard. The heating element in the heating base functions at a low wattage and is safe for your countertops.

Your **CROCK-POT®** slow cooker should be filled about one-half to three-fourths full for most recipes unless otherwise instructed. Lean meats such as chicken or pork tenderloin will cook faster than meats with more connective tissue and fat such as beef chuck or pork shoulder. Bone-in meats will take longer than boneless cuts. Typical **CROCK-POT®** slow cooker dishes take approximately 7 to 8 hours to reach the simmer point on LOW and about 3 to 4 hours on HIGH. Once the vegetables and meat start to simmer and braise, their flavors will fully blend and meat will become fall-off-the-bone tender.

According to the U.S. Department of Agriculture, all bacteria are killed at a temperature of 165°F. It's important to follow the recommended cooking times and not to open the lid often, especially early in the cooking process when heat is building up inside the unit. If you need to open the lid to check on your food or are adding additional ingredients, remember to allow additional cooking time if necessary to ensure food is cooked through and tender.

Large **CROCK-POT®** slow cookers, the 6- to 7-quart sizes, may benefit from a quick stir halfway through cook time to help distribute heat and promote even cooking. It's usually unnecessary to stir at all, as even ½ cup liquid will help to distribute heat, and the stoneware is the perfect medium for holding food at an even temperature throughout the cooking process.

OVEN-SAFE STONEWARE

All **CROCK-POT®** slow cooker removable stoneware inserts may (without their lids) be used safely in ovens at up to 400°F. In addition, all **CROCK-POT®** slow cookers are microwavable without their lids. If you own another slow cooker brand, please refer to your owner's manual for specific stoneware cooking medium tolerances.

FROZEN FOOD

Frozen food can be successfully cooked in a **CROCK-POT®** slow cooker. However, it will require longer cooking time than the same recipe made with fresh food. Using an instant-read thermometer is recommended to ensure meat is fully cooked.

PASTA AND RICE

If you are converting a recipe for your **CROCK-POT®** slow cooker that calls for uncooked pasta, first cook the pasta on the stovetop just until slightly tender. Then add the pasta to the **CROCK-POT®** slow cooker.

If you are converting a recipe for the **CROCK-POT®** slow cooker that calls for cooked rice, stir in raw rice with the other recipe ingredients plus ¼ cup extra liquid per ¼ cup of raw rice.

BEANS

Beans must be softened completely before combining with sugar and/or acidic foods in the **CROCK-POT®** slow cooker. Sugar and acid have a hardening effect on beans and will prevent softening. Fully cooked canned beans may be used as a substitute for dried beans.

VEGETABLES

Root vegetables often cook more slowly than meat. Cut vegetables accordingly to cook at the same rate as meat—large or small or lean versus marbled—and place near the sides or bottom of the stoneware to facilitate cooking.

HERBS

Fresh herbs add flavor and color when added at the end of the cooking cycle; if added at the beginning, many fresh herbs' flavor will dissipate over long cook times. Ground and/or dried herbs and spices work well in slow cooking and may be added at the beginning of cook time. For dishes with shorter cook times, hearty fresh herbs such as rosemary and thyme hold up well. The flavor power of all herbs and spices can vary greatly depending on their particular strength and shelf life. Use chili powders and garlic powder sparingly, as these can sometimes intensify over the long cook times. Always taste the finished dish and correct seasonings including salt and pepper.

LIQUIDS

It is not necessary to use more than ½ to 1 cup liquid in most instances. Most juices in meats and vegetables are retained more in slow cooking than in conventional cooking. Excess liquid can be cooked down and concentrated after slow cooking, either on the stovetop or by removing the meat and vegetables from the stoneware. Then stirring in one of the following thickeners and setting the **CROCK-POT®** slow cooker to HIGH. Cover and cook the liquid on HIGH for approximately 15 minutes or until thickened.

FLOUR: All-purpose flour is often used to thicken soups or stews. Stir water into the flour in a small bowl until smooth. With the **CROCK-POT®** slow cooker on HIGH, whisk flour mixture into the liquid in the **CROCK-POT®** slow cooker. Cover; cook on HIGH 15 minutes or until the mixture is thickened.

CORNSTARCH: Cornstarch gives sauces a clear, shiny appearance; it's used most often for sweet dessert sauces and stir-fry sauces. Stir water into the cornstarch in a small bowl until the cornstarch is dissolved. Quickly stir this mixture into the liquid in the **CROCK-POT®** slow cooker; the sauce will thicken as soon as the liquid simmers. Cornstarch breaks down with too much heat, so never add it at the beginning of the slow cooking process and turn off the heat as soon as the sauce thickens.

MILK

Milk, cream and sour cream break down during extended cooking. When possible, add them during the last 15 to 30 minutes of slow cooking, until just heated through. Condensed soups may be substituted for milk and may cook for extended times.

FISH

Fish is delicate and should be stirred into the **CROCK-POT**® slow cooker gently during the last 15 to 30 minutes of cooking. Cover; cook just until cooked through and serve immediately.

BAKED GOODS

If you wish to prepare bread, cakes or pudding cakes in a **CROCK-POT**® slow cooker, you may want to purchase a covered, vented metal cake pan accessory for your **CROCK-POT**® slow cooker. You can also use any straight-sided soufflé dish or deep cake pan that will fit into the stoneware of your unit. Baked goods can be prepared directly in the stoneware; however, they can be a little difficult to remove from the insert, so follow the recipe directions carefully.

MEXICAN
CHOCOLATE
BREAD PUDDING
P. 176

ZESTY APPETIZERS

MINI CARNITAS TACOS

Makes 12 servings

1½ pounds boneless pork loin, cubed

1 onion, finely chopped

½ cup chicken broth

1 tablespoon chili powder

2 teaspoons ground cumin

1 teaspoon dried oregano

½ teaspoon minced canned chipotle peppers in adobo sauce

½ cup pico de gallo

2 tablespoons chopped fresh cilantro

½ teaspoon salt

12 (6-inch) corn or flour tortillas

¾ cup (3 ounces) shredded sharp Cheddar cheese

3 tablespoons sour cream

1. Combine pork, onion, broth, chili powder, cumin, oregano and chipotle peppers in **CROCK-POT®** slow cooker; stir to blend. Cover; cook on LOW 6 hours or on HIGH 3 hours. Pour off excess cooking liquid.

2. Remove pork to large cutting board; shred with two forks. Return to **CROCK-POT®** slow cooker. Stir in pico de gallo, cilantro and salt. Cover; keep warm on LOW or WARM setting.

3. Cut three circles from each tortilla with 2-inch biscuit cutter. Top each with pork, cheese and sour cream. Serve warm.

TIP: Carnitas, or "little meats" in Spanish, are a festive way to spice up any gathering. Carnitas traditionally include a large amount of lard, but slow cooking makes the dish healthier by eliminating the need to add lard, oil or fat, while keeping the meat tender and delicious.

FIRECRACKER BLACK BEAN DIP

Makes about 3 cups

1 **can (15 ounces) refried black beans**

¾ **cup salsa**

1 **poblano pepper or 2 jalapeño peppers, seeded and minced***

1 **teaspoon chili powder**

½ **cup crumbled queso fresco****

3 **green onions, sliced**

Tortilla chips

Poblano peppers can sting and irritate the skin, so wear rubber gloves when handling peppers and do not touch your eyes.

**Queso fresco is a mild white Mexican cheese. If unavailable, you may substitute shredded Monterey Jack or Cheddar cheese.*

Combine beans, salsa, poblano pepper and chili powder in 2-quart **CROCK-POT®** slow cooker. Cover; cook on LOW 3 to 4 hours or on HIGH 2 hours. Top with queso fresco and green onions. Serve warm with tortilla chips.

CHIPOTLE CHILI CON QUESO DIP

Makes 1½ cups

10 **ounces pasteurized process cheese product, cubed**

¼ **cup mild chunky salsa**

½ **canned chipotle pepper in adobo sauce, finely chopped***

½ **teaspoon Worcestershire sauce**

⅛ **teaspoon chili powder**

Tortilla chips

Use more to taste.

Coat inside of **CROCK-POT®** "No Dial" slow cooker with nonstick cooking spray. Combine cheese product, salsa, chipotle pepper, Worcestershire sauce and chili powder in **CROCK-POT®** "No Dial" slow cooker; stir to blend. Cover; heat 1 hour. Stir. Cover; heat 30 minutes or until cheese product is melted. Stir. Serve with tortilla chips.

FIRECRACKER
BLACK BEAN DIP

SALSA-STYLE WINGS

Makes 4 servings

2 tablespoons vegetable oil

1½ pounds chicken wings (about 18 wings)

2 cups salsa

¼ cup packed brown sugar

Sprigs fresh cilantro (optional)

1. Heat oil in large skillet over medium-high heat. Add wings in batches; cook 3 to 4 minutes or until browned on all sides. Remove to **CROCK-POT®** slow cooker.

2. Combine salsa and brown sugar in medium bowl; stir to blend. Pour over wings. Cover; cook on LOW 5 to 6 hours or on HIGH 2 to 3 hours. Serve with salsa mixture. Garnish with cilantro.

CHUNKY PINTO BEAN DIP

Makes about 5 cups

2 cans (about 15 ounces *each*) pinto beans, rinsed and drained

1 can (about 14 ounces) diced tomatoes with mild green chiles

1 cup chopped onion

⅔ cup chunky salsa

1 tablespoon vegetable oil

1½ teaspoons minced garlic

1 teaspoon ground coriander

1 teaspoon ground cumin

1½ cups (6 ounces) shredded Mexican cheese blend or Cheddar cheese

¼ cup chopped fresh cilantro

Blue corn or other tortilla chips

1. Combine beans, tomatoes, onion, salsa, oil, garlic, coriander and cumin in **CROCK-POT®** slow cooker; stir to blend. Cover; cook on LOW 5 to 6 hours or until onion is tender.

2. Partially mash bean mixture with potato masher. Stir in cheese blend and cilantro. Serve with tortilla chips.

NACHO DIP

Makes 10 cups

1 tablespoon vegetable oil

1 onion, chopped

2 pounds ground beef

2 cans (about 15 ounces *each*) black beans, rinsed and drained

1 can (28 ounces) diced tomatoes

1 can (about 15 ounces) refried beans

1 can (about 15 ounces) cream-style corn

3 cloves garlic, minced

1 package (1¼ ounces) taco seasoning mix

Tortilla chips

Queso blanco

1. Heat oil in large skillet over medium-high heat. Add onion; cook 2 to 3 minutes or until translucent. Add beef; brown 6 to 8 minutes, stirring to break up meat. Drain fat.

2. Stir beef mixture, black beans, tomatoes, refried beans, corn, garlic and taco seasoning mix into **CROCK-POT®** slow cooker. Cover; cook on LOW 5 to 6 hours or on HIGH 2½ to 3 hours. Serve on tortilla chips. Sprinkle with queso blanco.

CHIPOTLE TURKEY SLOPPY JOE SLIDERS

Makes 12 sliders

1 pound turkey Italian sausage, casings removed

1 package (14 ounces) frozen green and red bell pepper strips with onions

1 can (6 ounces) tomato paste

1 tablespoon quick-cooking tapioca

1 tablespoon minced canned chipotle peppers in adobo sauce, plus 1 tablespoon sauce

2 teaspoons ground cumin

½ teaspoon dried thyme

12 corn muffins or small dinner rolls, split and toasted

1. Brown sausage in large skillet over medium-high heat 6 to 8 minutes, stirring to break up meat. Remove to **CROCK-POT®** slow cooker using slotted spoon.

2. Stir in pepper strips with onions, tomato paste, tapioca, chipotle peppers with sauce, cumin and thyme. Cover; cook on LOW 8 to 10 hours. Serve on corn muffins.

EASY TACO DIP

Makes about 3 cups

½ pound ground beef

1 cup frozen corn

½ cup chopped onion

½ cup salsa

½ cup mild taco sauce

1 can (4 ounces) diced mild green chiles, drained

1 can (4 ounces) sliced black olives, drained

1 cup (4 ounces) shredded Mexican cheese blend

Sour cream (optional)

Tortilla chips

1. Brown beef in large skillet over medium-high heat 6 to 8 minutes, stirring to break up meat. Remove beef to **CROCK-POT®** slow cooker using slotted spoon.

2. Add corn, onion, salsa, taco sauce, chiles and olives to **CROCK-POT®** slow cooker; stir to blend. Cover; cook on LOW 2 to 3 hours.

3. Just before serving, stir in cheese blend. Top with sour cream, if desired. Serve with tortilla chips.

TIP: To keep this dip hot through an entire party, simply leave it in the **CROCK-POT®** slow cooker on LOW or WARM.

CHICKEN MEATBALLS WITH CHIPOTLE-HONEY SAUCE

Makes 12 servings

2 pounds ground chicken

2 eggs, lightly beaten

⅓ cup plain dry bread crumbs

⅓ cup chopped fresh cilantro

3 tablespoons lime juice, divided

4 cloves garlic, minced

1 can (4 ounces) chipotle peppers in adobo sauce, divided

1½ teaspoons salt, divided

¾ cup honey

⅓ cup chicken broth

⅓ cup tomato paste

2 teaspoons Dijon mustard

1 tablespoon vegetable oil, plus additional as needed

1. Spray two medium baking sheets with nonstick cooking spray. Combine chicken, eggs, bread crumbs, cilantro, 2 tablespoons lime juice, garlic, 1 tablespoon adobo sauce and 1 teaspoon salt in large bowl. Shape into 48 meatballs. Place meatballs in single layer on prepared baking sheets. Cover with plastic wrap; refrigerate 1 hour.

2. Combine 2 to 3 chipotle peppers, honey, broth, tomato paste, mustard, remaining 1 tablespoon lime juice and ½ teaspoon salt in blender or food processor; blend until smooth. Pour sauce into **CROCK-POT®** slow cooker.

3. Heat 1 tablespoon oil in large skillet over medium-high heat. Working in batches, brown meatballs on all sides, adding additional oil as needed. Remove meatballs to **CROCK-POT®** slow cooker; stir gently to coat. Cover; cook on HIGH 3 to 4 hours or until meatballs are no longer pink in centers.

REFRIED BEAN DIP WITH BLUE TORTILLA CHIPS

Makes 10 servings

3 cans (about 16 ounces *each*) refried beans

1 cup prepared taco sauce

½ teaspoon salt

½ teaspoon black pepper

3 cups (12 ounces) shredded Cheddar cheese

¾ cup chopped green onions

2 packages (12 ounces *each*) blue tortilla chips

1. Combine refried beans, taco sauce, salt and pepper in large bowl; stir to blend. Spread one third of bean mixture on bottom of **CROCK-POT®** slow cooker. Sprinkle evenly with ¾ cup cheese. Repeat layers two times, finishing with cheese layer.

2. Sprinkle green onions evenly on cheese. Cover; cook on LOW 2 to 4 hours. Serve with tortilla chips.

BLACK BEAN AND MUSHROOM CHILAQUILES

Makes 6 servings

2 tablespoons olive oil

1 medium onion, chopped

1 medium green bell pepper, chopped

1 jalapeño or serrano pepper, seeded and minced*

2 cans (about 15 ounces *each*) black beans, rinsed and drained

1 can (about 14 ounces) diced tomatoes

10 ounces white mushrooms, cut into quarters

1½ teaspoons ground cumin

1½ teaspoons dried oregano

1 cup (4 ounces) shredded sharp white Cheddar cheese, plus additional for garnish

6 cups baked tortilla chips

Jalapeño and serrano peppers can sting and irritate the skin, so wear rubber gloves when handling peppers and do not touch your eyes.

1. Heat oil in medium skillet over medium heat. Add onion, bell pepper and jalapeño pepper; cook and stir 5 minutes or until onion is softened. Remove to **CROCK-POT®** slow cooker. Add beans, tomatoes, mushrooms, cumin and oregano.

2. Cover; cook on LOW 6 hours or on HIGH 3 hours. Sprinkle 1 cup Cheddar cheese over beans and mushrooms. Cover; cook on HIGH 15 minutes or until cheese is melted. Stir to combine.

3. For each serving, coarsely crush 1 cup tortilla chips into individual serving bowls. Top with black bean mixture. Garnish with additional cheese.

HOT SAUCED DRUMMETTES

Makes 8 servings

4 pounds chicken wing drummettes

2 teaspoons creole seasoning

⅛ teaspoon black pepper

2½ cups hot pepper sauce

¼ cup vegetable oil

¼ cup vinegar

4 teaspoons honey

1 teaspoon red pepper flakes

1 cup blue cheese dressing

Fresh celery stalks

1. Preheat broiler. Place drummettes on rack in broiler pan; season with creole seasoning and black pepper. Broil 4 to 5 inches from heat 10 to 12 minutes or until browned, turning once. Remove wings to **CROCK-POT®** slow cooker using slotted spoon.

2. Combine hot pepper sauce, oil, vinegar, honey and red pepper flakes in medium bowl; stir to blend. Pour over drummettes in **CROCK-POT®** slow cooker. Cover; cook on LOW 5 to 6 hours. Serve with dressing and celery.

FIESTA DIP

Makes 16 servings

8 ounces canned refried beans

½ cup (2 ounces) shredded Cheddar cheese, plus additional for garnish

⅓ cup chopped green chile pepper (optional)*

¼ cup salsa

Tortilla or corn chips

Chopped fresh tomatoes

Chile peppers can sting and irritate the skin, so wear rubber gloves when handling peppers and do not touch your eyes.

Combine beans, ½ cup cheese, chile pepper, if desired, and salsa in **CROCK-POT®** "No Dial" slow cooker. Cover; heat 45 minutes or until cheese is melted, stirring occasionally. Serve on tortilla chips. Garnish with tomatoes and additional cheese.

HOT SAUCED
DRUMMETTES

SIMMERING SOUPS

MEXICAN CHEESE SOUP

Makes 6 to 8 servings

1 pound ground beef

1 pound pasteurized process cheese product, cubed

1 can (about 15 ounces) kidney beans, rinsed and drained

1 can (about 14 ounces) diced tomatoes with mild green chiles

1 can (about 14 ounces) stewed tomatoes, undrained

1 can (8¾ ounces) corn

1 package (1¼ ounces) taco seasoning mix

1 jalapeño pepper, seeded and diced (optional)*

Tortilla chips (optional)

*Jalapeño peppers can sting and irritate the skin, so wear rubber gloves when handling peppers and do not touch your eyes.

1. Coat inside of **CROCK-POT®** slow cooker with nonstick cooking spray. Brown beef in large skillet 6 to 8 minutes, stirring to break up meat. Remove to **CROCK-POT®** slow cooker using slotted spoon.

2. Add cheese product, beans, tomatoes with chiles, stewed tomatoes, corn, taco seasoning mix and jalapeño pepper, if desired; stir to blend. Cover; cook on LOW 4 to 5 hours or on HIGH 3 hours. Serve with chips, if desired.

POZOLE ROJO

Makes 8 servings

4 dried ancho chiles, stemmed and seeded

3 dried guajillo chiles, stemmed and seeded*

2 cups boiling water

2½ pounds boneless pork shoulder, trimmed and cut in half

3 teaspoons salt, divided

1 tablespoon vegetable oil

2 medium onions, chopped

1½ tablespoons minced garlic

2 teaspoons ground cumin

2 teaspoons Mexican oregano**

4 cups chicken broth

2 cans (30 ounces *each*) white hominy, rinsed and drained

Optional toppings: sliced radishes, lime wedges, sliced romaine lettuce, chopped onion, tortilla chips and/or diced avocado

Guajillo chiles can be found in the ethnic section of large supermarkets.

**Mexican oregano has a stronger flavor than regular oregano. It can be found in the spices and seasonings section of most large supermarkets.*

1. Place ancho and guajillo chiles in medium bowl; pour boiling water over top. Weigh down chiles with small plate or bowl; soak 30 minutes.

2. Meanwhile, season pork with 1 teaspoon salt. Heat oil in large skillet over medium-high heat. Add pork; cook 8 to 10 minutes or until browned on all sides. Remove to **CROCK-POT®** slow cooker.

3. Heat same skillet over medium heat. Add onions; cook 6 minutes or until softened. Add garlic, cumin, oregano and remaining 2 teaspoons salt; cook and stir 1 minute. Stir in broth; bring to a simmer, scraping up any browned bits from bottom of skillet. Pour over pork in **CROCK-POT®** slow cooker.

4. Place softened chiles and soaking liquid in food processor or blender; blend until smooth. Pour through fine-mesh sieve into medium bowl, pressing with spoon to extract liquid. Discard solids. Stir mixture into **CROCK-POT®** slow cooker.

5. Cover; cook on LOW 5 hours. Stir in hominy. Cover; cook on LOW 1 hour. Turn off heat. Let stand 10 to 15 minutes. Skim off fat and discard. Remove pork to large cutting board; shred with two forks. Ladle hominy mixture into bowls; top each serving with pork and desired toppings.

FRESH LIME AND BLACK BEAN SOUP

Makes 4 servings

2 cans (about 15 ounces *each*) black beans, undrained

1 can (about 14 ounces) vegetable broth

1½ cups chopped onions

1½ teaspoons chili powder

¾ teaspoon ground cumin

¼ teaspoon garlic powder

⅛ to ¼ teaspoon red pepper flakes

½ cup sour cream

2 tablespoons extra virgin olive oil

2 tablespoons chopped fresh cilantro

1 medium lime, cut into wedges

1. Coat inside of **CROCK-POT®** slow cooker with nonstick cooking spray. Add beans, broth, onions, chili powder, cumin, garlic powder and red pepper flakes. Cover; cook on LOW 7 hours or on HIGH 3½ hours or until onions are very soft.

2. Process 1 cup soup mixture in food processor or blender until smooth. Return soup mixture to **CROCK-POT®** slow cooker. Stir, check consistency and repeat with additional 1 cup soup mixture as desired. Turn off heat. Let stand 15 to 20 minutes before serving.

3. Ladle soup into bowls. Divide sour cream, oil and cilantro evenly among servings. Squeeze juice from lime wedges over each.

TIP: Brighten the flavor of dishes cooked in the **CROCK-POT®** slow cooker by adding fresh herbs or fresh lime juice before serving.

CHICKEN FIESTA SOUP

Makes 8 servings

4 boneless, skinless chicken breasts, cooked and shredded

1 can (about 14 ounces) stewed tomatoes, drained

2 cans (4 ounces *each*) chopped mild green chiles

1 can (28 ounces) enchilada sauce

1 can (about 14 ounces) chicken broth

1 cup finely chopped onion

2 cloves garlic, minced

1 teaspoon ground cumin

1 teaspoon chili powder

1 teaspoon salt

¾ teaspoon black pepper

¼ cup finely chopped fresh cilantro

1 cup frozen corn

1 yellow squash, diced

1 zucchini, diced

8 tostada shells, crumbled

2 cups (8 ounces) shredded Cheddar cheese

Combine chicken, tomatoes, chiles, enchilada sauce, broth, onion, garlic, cumin, chili powder, salt, pepper, cilantro, corn, squash and zucchini in **CROCK-POT®** slow cooker; stir to blend. Cover; cook on LOW 8 hours. Top each serving with crumbled tostada shells and cheese.

BEEF FAJITA SOUP

Makes 8 servings

1 pound cubed beef stew meat

1 can (about 15 ounces) pinto beans, rinsed and drained

1 can (about 15 ounces) black beans, rinsed and drained

1 can (about 14 ounces) diced tomatoes with roasted garlic

1 can (about 14 ounces) beef broth

1½ cups water

1 green bell pepper, thinly sliced

1 red bell pepper, thinly sliced

1 onion, thinly sliced

2 teaspoons ground cumin

1 teaspoon seasoned salt

1 teaspoon black pepper

Optional toppings: sour cream, shredded cheese and/or chopped olives

Combine beef, beans, tomatoes, broth, water, bell peppers, onion, cumin, seasoned salt and black pepper in **CROCK-POT®** slow cooker; stir to blend. Cover; cook on LOW 8 hours. Top as desired.

HEARTY TORTILLA SOUP

Makes 4 to 6 servings

2 cans (about 14 ounces *each*) diced tomatoes

1 can (4 ounces) diced mild green chiles, drained

1 cup chicken broth, divided

1 yellow onion, diced

2 cloves garlic, minced

1 teaspoon ground cumin

4 boneless, skinless chicken thighs

Salt and black pepper

4 corn tortillas, sliced into ¼-inch strips

2 tablespoons chopped fresh cilantro

½ cup (2 ounces) shredded Monterey Jack cheese

1 avocado, diced and tossed with lime juice

Lime wedges

1. Combine tomatoes, chiles, ½ cup broth, onion, garlic and cumin in **CROCK-POT®** slow cooker; stir to blend. Add chicken. Cover; cook on LOW 6 hours or on HIGH 3 hours.

2. Remove chicken to large cutting board; shred with two forks. Return to cooking liquid. Season with salt, pepper and additional ½ cup broth, if necessary.

3. Just before serving, add tortillas and cilantro to **CROCK-POT®** slow cooker; stir to blend. Top each serving with cheese, avocado and lime juice.

BLACK BEAN CHIPOTLE SOUP

Makes 4 to 6 servings

1 pound dried black beans, rinsed and sorted

6 cups chicken or vegetable broth

1 large onion, chopped

1 cup crushed tomatoes

2 stalks celery, diced

2 carrots, diced

1 can (4 ounces) diced mild green chiles, drained

2 canned chipotle peppers in adobo sauce, chopped

2 teaspoons ground cumin

Salt and black pepper

Optional toppings: sour cream, pico de gallo and/or chopped fresh cilantro

1. Place beans in large bowl; cover completely with water. Soak 6 to 8 hours or overnight.* Drain beans; discard water.

2. Place beans in **CROCK-POT®** slow cooker. Add broth, onion, tomatoes, celery, carrots, chiles, chipotle peppers and cumin; stir to blend.

3. Cover; cook on LOW 7 to 8 hours or on HIGH 4½ to 5 hours. Season with salt and black pepper. Place mixture in batches in food processor or blender; process to desired consistency. Top as desired.

*To quick soak beans, place beans in large saucepan. Cover with water; bring to a boil over high heat. Boil 2 minutes. Remove from heat; let soak, covered, 1 hour.

VARIATION: For an even heartier soup, add 1 cup diced browned spicy sausage, such as linguiça or chourico.

HEARTY CHICKEN TEQUILA SOUP

Makes 4 servings

1 small onion, cut into 8 wedges

1 cup frozen corn

1 can (about 14 ounces) diced tomatoes with mild green chiles

2 cloves garlic, minced

2 tablespoons chopped fresh cilantro, plus additional for garnish

1 whole fryer chicken (about 3½ pounds)

2 cups chicken broth

3 tablespoons tequila

¼ cup sour cream

1. Place onion wedges on bottom of **CROCK-POT®** slow cooker. Add corn, tomatoes, garlic and 2 tablespoons cilantro; stir to blend. Place chicken on top of tomato mixture.

2. Pour broth and tequila over chicken and tomato mixture. Cover; cook on LOW 8 to 10 hours.

3. Remove chicken to large cutting board; discard skin and bones. Shred chicken with two forks. Stir shredded chicken back into **CROCK-POT®** slow cooker. Top each serving with dollop of sour cream and garnish with additional cilantro.

MEXICAN CHICKEN AND BLACK BEAN SOUP

Makes 4 servings

4 bone-in chicken thighs, skin removed

1 cup finely chopped onion

1 can (about 14 ounces) chicken broth

1 can (about 14 ounces) diced tomatoes with Mexican seasoning or diced tomatoes with mild green chiles

1 can (about 15 ounces) black beans, rinsed and drained

1 cup frozen corn

1 can (4 ounces) chopped mild green chiles

1 tablespoon chili powder

1 teaspoon salt

1 teaspoon ground cumin

Optional toppings: sour cream, sliced avocado, shredded cheese, chopped fresh cilantro and/or fried tortilla strips

1. Coat inside of **CROCK-POT®** slow cooker with nonstick cooking spray. Combine chicken, onion, broth, tomatoes, beans, corn, chiles, chili powder, salt and cumin in **CROCK-POT®** slow cooker; stir to blend. Cover; cook on HIGH 3 to 4 hours or until chicken is cooked through.

2. Remove chicken to large cutting board using slotted spoon. Discard bones and chop chicken. Stir chicken back into **CROCK-POT®** slow cooker. Serve in bowls. Top as desired.

POSOLE

Makes 8 servings

3 pounds boneless pork shoulder roast, cubed

2 cans (about 15 ounces *each*) white hominy, rinsed and drained

1 package (10 ounces) frozen white corn, thawed

1 cup chili sauce

Combine pork, hominy, corn and chili sauce in **CROCK-POT®** slow cooker; stir to blend. Cover; cook on LOW 10 hours or on HIGH 5 hours.

WHITE BEAN AND GREEN CHILE PEPPER SOUP

Makes 5 servings

2 cans (about 15 ounces *each*) Great Northern beans, rinsed and drained

1 can (about 14 ounces) vegetable broth

1 cup finely chopped yellow onion

1 can (4 ounces) diced mild green chiles

1 teaspoon ground cumin, divided

½ teaspoon garlic powder

¼ cup chopped fresh cilantro

1 tablespoon olive oil

Sour cream (optional)

Combine beans, broth, onion, chiles, ½ teaspoon cumin and garlic powder in **CROCK-POT®** slow cooker. Cover; cook on LOW 8 hours or on HIGH 4 hours. Stir in cilantro, oil and remaining ½ teaspoon cumin. Garnish with sour cream, if desired.

POSOLE

FIESTA BLACK BEAN SOUP

Makes 6 to 8 servings

6 cups chicken broth

¾ cup diced potatoes

1 can (about 15 ounces) black beans, rinsed and drained

½ pound cooked ham, chopped

½ onion, chopped

1 can (4 ounces) diced mild green chiles

2 cloves garlic, minced

2 teaspoons dried oregano

1½ teaspoons dried thyme

1 teaspoon ground cumin

Optional toppings: sour cream, chopped bell pepper and chopped tomatoes

Combine broth, potatoes, beans, ham, onion, chiles, garlic, oregano, thyme and cumin in **CROCK-POT®** slow cooker; stir to blend. Cover; cook on LOW 8 to 10 hours or on HIGH 4 to 5 hours. Top as desired.

STEWS AND CHILIES

CHIPOTLE VEGETABLE CHILI WITH CHOCOLATE

Makes 6 servings

2 tablespoons olive oil

1 medium onion, chopped

1 medium green bell pepper, chopped

1 medium red bell pepper, chopped

1 cup frozen corn

1 can (28 ounces) diced tomatoes

1 can (about 15 ounces) black beans, rinsed and drained

1 can (about 15 ounces) pinto beans, rinsed and drained

1 tablespoon chili powder

1 teaspoon ground cumin

½ teaspoon chipotle chili powder

1 ounce semisweet chocolate, chopped

1. Heat oil in large skillet over medium-high heat. Add onion and bell peppers; cook and stir 4 minutes or until softened. Stir in corn; cook 3 minutes. Remove to **CROCK-POT®** slow cooker.

2. Stir tomatoes, beans, chili powder, cumin and chipotle chili powder into **CROCK-POT®** slow cooker. Cover; cook on LOW 6 to 7 hours. Stir chocolate into **CROCK-POT®** slow cooker until melted.

NEW MEXICAN GREEN CHILE PORK STEW

Makes 6 servings

1½ pounds boneless pork shoulder roast, cubed

2 medium baking potatoes or sweet potatoes, peeled and cut into 1-inch pieces

1 cup chopped onion

1 cup frozen corn

1 can (4 ounces) diced mild green chiles

1 jar (16 ounces) salsa verde (green salsa)

2 teaspoons sugar

2 teaspoons ground cumin or chili powder

1 teaspoon dried oregano

Hot cooked rice

¼ cup chopped fresh cilantro (optional)

1. Place pork, potatoes, onion, corn and chiles in **CROCK-POT®** slow cooker. Combine salsa, sugar, cumin and oregano in small bowl; stir to blend. Pour over pork and vegetables.

2. Cover; cook on LOW 6 to 8 hours or on HIGH 4 to 5 hours or until pork is tender. Serve stew with rice; garnish with cilantro.

SWEET POTATO AND BLACK BEAN CHIPOTLE CHILI

Makes 8 to 10 servings

1 tablespoon vegetable oil

2 large onions, diced

3 tablespoons chili powder

2 tablespoons tomato paste

1 tablespoon minced garlic

1 tablespoon chipotle chili powder

2 teaspoons kosher salt

1 teaspoon ground cumin

1 cup water

2 large sweet potatoes, peeled and cut into ½-inch pieces (about 2 pounds)

2 cans (28 ounces *each*) crushed tomatoes

2 cans (about 15 ounces *each*) black beans, rinsed and drained

Optional toppings: sliced green onions, shredded Cheddar cheese and/or tortilla chips

1. Heat oil in large skillet over medium-high heat. Add onions; cook 8 minutes or until lightly browned and softened. Add chili powder, tomato paste, garlic, chipotle chili powder, salt and cumin; cook and stir 1 minute. Add water, stirring to scrape up any brown bits from bottom of skillet. Remove to **CROCK-POT®** slow cooker. Add sweet potatoes, tomatoes and beans.

2. Cover; cook on LOW 8 hours or on HIGH 4 hours. Ladle into individual bowls. Top with desired toppings.

CHILI VERDE

Makes 4 servings

Nonstick cooking spray

¾ pound boneless pork shoulder roast, cubed

1 pound tomatillos, husks removed, rinsed and coarsely chopped

1 can (about 15 ounces) Great Northern beans, rinsed and drained

1 can (about 14 ounces) chicken broth

1 onion, halved and thinly sliced

1 can (4 ounces) diced mild green chiles

6 cloves garlic, chopped or sliced

1 teaspoon ground cumin

Salt and black pepper

½ cup lightly packed fresh cilantro, chopped

Sour cream

1. Spray large skillet with cooking spray; heat over medium-high heat. Add pork; cook 6 to 8 minutes or until browned on all sides. Remove to **CROCK-POT®** slow cooker.

2. Add tomatillos, beans, broth, onion, chiles, garlic, cumin, salt and pepper to **CROCK-POT®** slow cooker; stir to blend. Cover; cook on HIGH 3 to 4 hours or until pork is fork-tender.

3. Turn **CROCK-POT®** slow cooker to LOW. Stir in cilantro. Cover; cook on LOW 10 minutes. Serve with sour cream.

CHILI CON QUESO

Makes 3 cups

1 package (16 ounces) pasteurized process cheese product, cubed

1 can (10 ounces) diced tomatoes with mild green chiles

1 cup sliced green onions

2 teaspoons ground coriander

2 teaspoons ground cumin

¾ teaspoon hot pepper sauce

Green onion strips (optional)

Jalapeño pepper slices (optional)*

Tortilla chips

Jalapeño peppers can sting and irritate the skin, so wear rubber gloves when handling peppers and do not touch your eyes.

1. Combine cheese product, tomatoes, green onions, coriander, cumin and hot pepper sauce in 1½-quart **CROCK-POT®** slow cooker; stir until well blended.

2. Cover; cook on LOW 2 hours or until heated through. Garnish with green onion strips and jalapeño pepper slices, if desired. Serve with tortilla chips.

SERVING SUGGESTION: Serve Chili con Queso with pita chips. Cut pita bread rounds into triangles and toast them in a preheated 400°F oven 5 minutes or until crisp.

CHORIZO CHILI

Makes 6 servings

1 pound ground beef

8 ounces bulk raw chorizo sausage or ½ (15-ounce) package raw chorizo sausage, casings removed*

1 can (about 15 ounces) chili beans in chili sauce

2 cans (about 14 ounces *each*) chili-style diced tomatoes

Optional toppings: sour cream, fresh chives and shredded Cheddar cheese

A highly seasoned Mexican pork sausage.

1. Brown beef and chorizo in large skillet over medium-high heat 6 to 8 minutes, stirring to break up meat. Remove beef mixture to **CROCK-POT®** slow cooker using slotted spoon. Stir beans and tomatoes into **CROCK-POT®** slow cooker.

2. Cover; cook on LOW 7 hours. Turn off heat. Let stand 10 to 12 minutes. Skim fat from surface. Top as desired.

MOLE CHILI

Makes 4 to 6 servings

2 corn tortillas, *each* cut into 4 wedges

1½ pounds beef chuck roast, cut into 1-inch pieces

¾ teaspoon salt

½ teaspoon black pepper

3 tablespoons olive oil, divided

2 medium onions, chopped

5 cloves garlic, minced

1 cup beef broth

1 can (about 14 ounces) fire-roasted diced tomatoes

2 tablespoons chili powder

1 tablespoon ground ancho chile

1 teaspoon ground cumin

1 teaspoon dried oregano

¾ teaspoon ground cinnamon

1 can (about 15 ounces) red kidney beans, rinsed and drained

2 ounces semisweet chocolate, chopped

Queso fresco (optional)

Chopped fresh cilantro (optional)

1. Coat inside of **CROCK-POT®** slow cooker with nonstick cooking spray. Place tortillas in food processor or blender; process to fine crumbs. Set aside.

2. Season beef with salt and pepper. Heat 1 tablespoon oil in large skillet over medium-high heat. Add half of beef to skillet; cook 4 minutes or until browned. Remove to **CROCK-POT®** slow cooker. Add 1 tablespoon oil to skillet and repeat with remaining beef. Heat remaining 1 tablespoon oil in skillet. Add onions and garlic; cook 2 minutes or until starting to soften. Pour broth into skillet, scraping up any browned bits from bottom of skillet. Remove to **CROCK-POT®** slow cooker. Stir in reserved tortilla crumbs, tomatoes, chili powder, ancho chile, cumin, oregano and cinnamon.

3. Cover; cook on LOW 8 to 8½ hours or on HIGH 4 to 4½ hours. Stir in beans. Cover; cook on LOW 30 minutes. Turn off heat. Add chocolate; stir until melted. Top with queso fresco and cilantro, if desired.

THREE-BEAN CHIPOTLE CHILI

Makes 6 servings

2 tablespoons olive oil

1 onion, chopped

1 green bell pepper, chopped

2 cloves garlic, minced

2 cans (about 15 ounces *each*) pinto or pink beans, rinsed and drained

1 can (about 15 ounces) small white beans, rinsed and drained

1 can (about 15 ounces) chickpeas, rinsed and drained

1 cup frozen or canned corn

1 cup water

1 can (6 ounces) tomato paste

1 or 2 canned chipotle peppers in adobo sauce, finely chopped

Salt and black pepper

Optional toppings: sour cream, shredded Cheddar cheese and chopped fresh chives (optional)

1. Heat oil in large skillet over medium heat. Add onion, bell pepper and garlic; cook and stir 3 to 5 minutes or until softened. Remove to **CROCK-POT®** slow cooker.

2. Stir beans, chickpeas, corn, water, tomato paste and chipotle peppers into **CROCK-POT®** slow cooker. Cover; cook on LOW 3½ to 4 hours. Top as desired.

CHIPOTLE CHICKEN STEW

Makes 6 servings

1 pound boneless, skinless chicken thighs, cubed

1 can (about 15 ounces) navy beans, rinsed and drained

1 can (about 15 ounces) black beans, rinsed and drained

1 can (about 14 ounces) crushed tomatoes, undrained

1½ cups chicken broth

½ cup orange juice

1 medium onion, diced

1 canned chipotle pepper in adobo sauce, minced

1 teaspoon salt

1 teaspoon ground cumin

1 whole bay leaf

Sprigs fresh cilantro (optional)

1. Combine chicken, beans, tomatoes, broth, orange juice, onion, chipotle pepper, salt, cumin and bay leaf in **CROCK-POT®** slow cooker; stir to blend.

2. Cover; cook on LOW 7 to 8 hours or on HIGH 3½ to 4 hours. Remove and discard bay leaf. Garnish with cilantro.

CHICKEN AND CHILE PEPPER STEW

Makes 6 servings

1 pound boneless, skinless chicken thighs, cut into ½-inch pieces

1 pound small potatoes, cut lengthwise into halves, then crosswise into slices

1 cup chopped yellow onion

2 poblano peppers, seeded and cut into ½-inch pieces*

1 jalapeño pepper, seeded and finely chopped*

3 cloves garlic, minced

3 cups chicken broth

1 can (about 14 ounces) diced tomatoes

2 tablespoons chili powder

1 teaspoon dried oregano

Poblano and jalapeño peppers can sting and irritate the skin, so wear rubber gloves when handling peppers and do not touch your eyes.

Combine chicken, potatoes, onion, poblano peppers, jalapeño pepper and garlic in **CROCK-POT®** slow cooker. Combine broth, tomatoes, chili powder and oregano in large bowl; stir to blend. Pour into **CROCK-POT®** slow cooker. Cover; cook on LOW 8 to 9 hours.

THREE-BEAN TURKEY CHILI

Makes 6 to 8 servings

1 pound ground turkey

1 small onion, chopped

1 can (28 ounces) diced tomatoes, undrained

1 can (about 15 ounces) chickpeas, rinsed and drained

1 can (about 15 ounces) kidney beans, rinsed and drained

1 can (about 15 ounces) black beans, rinsed and drained

1 can (8 ounces) tomato sauce

1 can (4 ounces) diced mild green chiles

1 to 2 tablespoons chili powder

Sprigs fresh cilantro (optional)

1. Heat large skillet over medium-high heat. Add turkey and onion; cook and stir 6 to 8 minutes. Drain fat. Remove turkey mixture to **CROCK-POT®** slow cooker.

2. Add tomatoes, chickpeas, beans, tomato sauce, chiles and chili powder to **CROCK-POT®** slow cooker; stir to blend. Cover; cook on HIGH 6 to 8 hours. Garnish with cilantro.

CHICKEN AND TURKEY

SHREDDED CHICKEN TACOS

Makes 4 servings

2 pounds boneless, skinless chicken thighs

½ cup prepared mango salsa, plus additional for serving

Lettuce (optional)

8 (6-inch) yellow corn tortillas, warmed

1. Coat inside of **CROCK-POT®** slow cooker with nonstick cooking spray. Add chicken and ½ cup salsa. Cover; cook on LOW 4 to 5 hours or on HIGH 2½ to 3 hours.

2. Remove chicken to large cutting board; shred with two forks. Stir shredded chicken back into **CROCK-POT®** slow cooker. To serve, divide chicken and lettuce, if desired, evenly among tortillas. Serve with additional salsa.

CERVEZA CHICKEN ENCHILADA CASSEROLE

Makes 4 to 6 servings

2 cups water

1 bottle (12 ounces) Mexican beer, divided

1 stalk celery, chopped

1 small carrot, chopped

Juice of 1 lime

1 teaspoon salt

1½ pounds boneless, skinless chicken breasts

1 can (about 10 ounces) enchilada sauce

1 bag (9 ounces) white corn tortilla chips

½ medium onion, chopped

3 cups (12 ounces) shredded Cheddar cheese

Sour cream and sliced olives (optional)

1. Place water, 1 cup beer, celery, carrot, lime juice and salt in large saucepan. Bring to a boil over high heat. Place chicken in saucepan; reduce heat to medium-low. Cook 12 to 14 minutes or until chicken is no longer pink in center. Remove chicken to large cutting board; shred with two forks.

2. Pour one third of enchilada sauce into **CROCK-POT®** slow cooker. Arrange one third of tortilla chips over sauce. Layer with one third of shredded chicken and one third of chopped onion. Sprinkle with 1 cup cheese. Repeat layers two more times, pouring remaining beer over casserole before adding last cup of cheese.

3. Cover; cook on LOW 3½ to 4 hours. Garnish with sour cream and olives.

CHIPOTLE CORNISH HENS

Makes 4 servings

3 small carrots, cut into ½-inch rounds

3 stalks celery, cut into ½-inch pieces

1 onion, chopped

1 can (7 ounces) chipotle peppers in adobo sauce, divided

2 cups prepared corn bread stuffing

4 Cornish hens (about 1½ pounds each)

Salt and black pepper

Sprigs fresh Italian parsley, (optional)

1. Coat inside of **CROCK-POT®** slow cooker with nonstick cooking spray. Add carrots, celery and onion.

2. Pour canned chipotles into small bowl. Finely chop ½ chipotle pepper; mix into prepared stuffing. Remove remaining peppers from adobo sauce and reserve for another use. Finely chop remaining ½ chipotle pepper and add to adobo sauce.*

3. Rinse and dry hens, removing giblets, if any. Season with salt and black pepper inside and out. Fill *each* hen with about ½ cup stuffing. Rub adobo sauce onto hens. Place in **CROCK-POT®** slow cooker, arranging hens necks down, legs up. Cover; cook on HIGH 3½ to 4 hours.

4. Remove hens to large serving platter. Remove vegetables using slotted spoon; arrange around hens. Garnish with parsley. Spoon cooking juices over hens and vegetables.

*For spicier flavor, use 1 chipotle pepper in stuffing and 1 chipotle pepper in sauce.

SPANISH PAELLA WITH CHICKEN AND SAUSAGE

Makes 4 servings

1 tablespoon olive oil

4 chicken thighs (about 2 pounds *total*)

1 onion, chopped

1 clove garlic, minced

4 cups chicken broth

1 pound hot smoked sausage, sliced into rounds

1 can (about 14 ounces) stewed tomatoes, undrained

1 cup uncooked Arborio rice

1 pinch saffron (optional)

½ cup frozen peas, thawed

1. Heat oil in large skillet over medium-high heat. Add chicken in batches; cook 6 to 8 minutes until browned on all sides. Remove to **CROCK-POT®** slow cooker.

2. Add onion to skillet; cook and stir 5 minutes or until translucent. Add garlic; cook and stir 30 seconds. Stir in broth, sausage, tomatoes, rice and saffron, if desired. Pour over chicken. Cover; cook on LOW 6 to 8 hours or on HIGH 3 to 4 hours or until chicken is cooked through and rice is tender.

3. Remove chicken pieces to large plate; fluff rice with fork. Stir in peas. Spoon rice into bowls; top with chicken.

SWEET JALAPEÑO MUSTARD TURKEY THIGHS

Makes 6 servings

6 turkey thighs, skin removed

¾ cup honey mustard

½ cup orange juice

1 tablespoon cider vinegar

1 teaspoon Worcestershire sauce

1 to 2 fresh jalapeño peppers, finely chopped*

1 clove garlic, minced

½ teaspoon grated orange peel

Jalapeño peppers can sting and irritate the skin, so wear rubber gloves when handling peppers and do not touch your eyes.

Place turkey thighs in single layer in **CROCK-POT®** slow cooker. Combine honey mustard, orange juice, cider vinegar, Worcestershire sauce, jalapeño pepper, garlic and orange peel in large bowl; stir to blend. Pour mixture over turkey thighs. Cover; cook on LOW 5 to 6 hours.

SOUTH-OF-THE-BORDER CUMIN CHICKEN

Makes 4 servings

1 package (16 ounces) frozen bell pepper stir-fry mixture, thawed *or* 3 bell peppers, thinly sliced*

4 chicken drumsticks, skin removed

4 chicken thighs, skin removed

1 can (about 14 ounces) stewed tomatoes

1 tablespoon green pepper sauce

2 teaspoons sugar

1¾ teaspoons ground cumin, divided

1¼ teaspoons salt

1 teaspoon dried oregano

¼ cup chopped fresh cilantro

1 to 2 medium limes, cut into wedges

Hot cooked rice (optional)

If using fresh bell peppers, add 1 small onion, chopped.

1. Place bell pepper mixture in **CROCK-POT®** slow cooker; arrange chicken on top of peppers.

2. Combine tomatoes, pepper sauce, sugar, 1 teaspoon cumin, salt and oregano in large bowl; stir to blend. Pour over chicken mixture. Cover; cook on LOW 8 hours or on HIGH 4 hours or until meat is just beginning to fall off bone.

3. Place chicken in shallow serving bowl. Stir remaining ¾ teaspoon cumin into tomato mixture; pour over chicken. Sprinkle with cilantro. Serve with lime wedges and cooked rice, if desired.

TURKEY ROPA VIEJA

Makes 4 servings

12 ounces turkey tenderloin (2 large or 3 small) or boneless, skinless chicken thighs

1 can (8 ounces) tomato sauce

2 medium tomatoes, chopped

1 small onion, thinly sliced

1 small green bell pepper, chopped

4 pimiento-stuffed green olives, sliced

1 clove garlic, minced

¾ teaspoon ground cumin

½ teaspoon dried oregano

⅛ teaspoon black pepper

2 teaspoons lemon juice

¼ teaspoon salt

Cooked rice and black beans (optional)

1. Place turkey in **CROCK-POT®** slow cooker. Add tomato sauce, tomatoes, onion, bell pepper, olives, garlic, cumin, oregano and black pepper. Cover; cook on LOW 6 to 7 hours.

2. Remove turkey to large cutting board; shred with two forks. Stir shredded turkey, lemon juice and salt into **CROCK-POT®** slow cooker. Serve with rice and black beans, if desired.

CHICKEN AZTECA

Makes 4 servings

2 cups frozen corn

1 can (about 15 ounces) black beans, rinsed and drained

1 cup chunky salsa, divided

1 clove garlic, minced

½ teaspoon ground cumin

4 boneless, skinless chicken breasts (about 1 pound)

1 package (8 ounces) cream cheese, cubed

Hot cooked rice

Shredded Cheddar cheese

1. Combine corn, beans, ½ cup salsa, garlic and cumin in **CROCK-POT®** slow cooker; stir to blend. Arrange chicken over top of corn mixture; pour remaining ½ cup salsa over chicken. Cover; cook on LOW 4 to 6 hours or on HIGH 2 to 3 hours.

2. Remove chicken to large cutting board; cut into 1-inch pieces. Return chicken to **CROCK-POT®** slow cooker. Add cream cheese. Cover; cook on HIGH 15 to 20 minutes or until cream cheese is melted and blends into sauce. Serve chicken and sauce over rice. Top with Cheddar cheese.

CHICKEN AND SPICY BLACK BEAN TACOS

Makes 4 servings

1 can (about 15 ounces) black beans, rinsed and drained

1 can (10 ounces) diced tomatoes with mild green chiles, drained

1½ teaspoons chili powder

¾ teaspoon ground cumin

1 tablespoon plus 1 teaspoon extra virgin olive oil, divided

12 ounces boneless, skinless chicken breasts

12 crisp corn taco shells

Lime and orange wedges (optional)

Optional toppings: shredded lettuce, diced tomatoes, shredded Cheddar cheese and/or sliced black olives

1. Coat inside of **CROCK-POT®** slow cooker with nonstick cooking spray. Add beans and tomatoes with chiles. Combine chili powder, cumin and 1 teaspoon oil in small bowl; rub onto chicken. Place chicken in **CROCK-POT®** slow cooker. Cover; cook on HIGH 1¾ hours.

2. Remove chicken to large cutting board; slice. Remove bean mixture to large bowl using slotted spoon. Stir in remaining 1 tablespoon oil.

3. To serve, warm taco shells according to package directions. Fill with equal amounts of bean mixture and chicken. Top as desired.

ZESTY CHICKEN
AND RICE SUPPER

Makes 2 to 4 servings

2 boneless, skinless chicken breasts, cut into 1-inch pieces

2 large green bell peppers, chopped

1 small onion, chopped

1 can (about 28 ounces) diced tomatoes, undrained

1 cup uncooked rice

1 cup water

1 package (1¼ ounces) taco seasoning mix

1 teaspoon salt

1 teaspoon black pepper

1 teaspoon ground red pepper

Sprigs fresh cilantro (optional)

Shredded Cheddar cheese (optional)

Combine chicken, bell peppers, onion, tomatoes, rice, water, taco seasoning mix, salt, black pepper and ground red pepper in **CROCK-POT®** slow cooker; stir to blend. Cover; cook on LOW 6 to 8 hours or on HIGH 3 to 4 hours. Garnish with cilantro. Top with cheese, if desired.

CHICKEN ENCHILADA ROLL-UPS

Makes 6 servings

1½ **pounds boneless, skinless chicken breasts**

½ **cup plus 2 tablespoons all-purpose flour, divided**

½ **teaspoon salt**

2 **tablespoons butter**

1 **cup chicken broth**

1 **small onion, diced**

¼ **to ½ cup canned jalapeño peppers,* sliced**

½ **teaspoon dried oregano**

2 **tablespoons whipping cream or milk**

6 **(7- to 8-inch) flour tortillas**

6 **thin slices American cheese or American cheese with jalapeño peppers**

*Jalapeño peppers can sting and irritate the skin, so wear rubber gloves when handling peppers and do not touch your eyes.

1. Cut each chicken breast lengthwise into 2 or 3 strips. Combine ½ cup flour and salt in large resealable food storage bag. Add chicken strips; shake to coat with flour mixture. Melt butter in large skillet over medium heat. Brown chicken strips in batches, 2 to 3 minutes per side. Remove chicken to **CROCK-POT®** slow cooker.

2. Add broth to skillet, scraping up any browned bits. Pour broth mixture into **CROCK-POT®** slow cooker. Add onion, jalapeño peppers and oregano. Cover; cook on LOW 7 to 8 hours or on HIGH 3 to 4 hours.

3. Blend remaining 2 tablespoons flour and cream in small bowl until smooth. Stir into chicken mixture. Cook, uncovered, on HIGH 15 minutes or until thickened. Spoon chicken mixture onto center of flour tortillas. Top with 1 cheese slice. Fold up tortillas and serve.

SERVING SUGGESTION: This rich, creamy chicken mixture can also be served over hot cooked rice.

BEEF AND PORK

FIERY SHREDDED BEEF TACOS

Makes 6 to 8 servings

1 boneless beef chuck roast
   (2½ pounds)

1¼ teaspoons salt, divided

1 teaspoon *each* cumin, garlic
   powder and smoked paprika

2 tablespoons olive oil, divided

2 cups beef broth

1 red bell pepper, sliced

1 tomato, cut into wedges

½ onion, sliced

2 cloves garlic, minced

1 to 2 canned chipotle peppers in
   adobo sauce

Juice of 1 lime

Corn or flour tortillas

Optional toppings: sliced bell
   peppers, avocado, diced onion,
   lime wedges and/or chopped
   fresh cilantro

1. Season beef with 1 teaspoon salt, cumin, garlic powder and smoked paprika. Heat 1 tablespoon oil in large skillet over medium-high heat. Add beef; cook 5 minutes on each side until browned. Remove to **CROCK-POT®** slow cooker.

2. Pour in broth. Cover; cook on LOW 8 to 9 hours or on HIGH 4 to 5 hours.

3. Meanwhile, preheat oven to 425°F. Combine bell pepper, tomato, onion and garlic on large baking sheet. Drizzle with remaining 1 tablespoon oil. Roast 40 minutes or until vegetables are tender. Place vegetables, chipotle pepper, lime juice and remaining ¼ teaspoon salt in food processor or blender; blend until smooth.

4. Remove beef to large cutting board; shred with two forks. Combine shredded meat with 1 cup cooking liquid. Discard remaining cooking liquid. Serve on tortillas with sauce. Top as desired.

PORK CHOPS WITH JALAPEÑO-PECAN CORN BREAD STUFFING

Makes 6 servings

6 boneless pork loin chops (1½ pounds), *each* 1 inch thick

Nonstick cooking spray

¾ cup chopped onion

¾ cup chopped celery

½ cup coarsely chopped pecans

½ jalapeño pepper, seeded and chopped*

1 teaspoon rubbed sage

½ teaspoon dried rosemary

⅛ teaspoon black pepper

4 cups unseasoned corn bread stuffing mix

1¼ cups chicken broth

1 egg, lightly beaten

Sprigs fresh rosemary (optional)

Jalapeño peppers can sting and irritate the skin, so wear rubber gloves when handling peppers and do not touch your eyes.

1. Trim excess fat from pork; discard. Spray large skillet with cooking spray; heat over medium heat. Add pork; cook 6 to 8 minutes or until browned on both sides. Remove to large plate.

2. Add onion, celery, pecans, jalapeño pepper, sage, dried rosemary and black pepper to skillet; cook and stir 5 minutes or until onion and celery are tender.

3. Combine stuffing mix, vegetable mixture and broth in medium bowl. Stir in egg. Spoon stuffing mixture into **CROCK-POT®** slow cooker. Arrange pork on top. Cover; cook on LOW 5 hours or until pork is tender and barely pink in center. Garnish each serving with rosemary sprig.

NOTE: If you prefer a more moist dressing, increase the chicken broth to 1½ cups.

BEEFY TOSTADA PIE

Makes 4 to 6 servings

2 teaspoons olive oil

1½ cups chopped onion

2 pounds ground beef

1 teaspoon salt

1 teaspoon ground cumin

1 teaspoon chili powder

2 cloves garlic, minced

1 can (15 ounces) tomato sauce

1 cup sliced black olives

8 (6-inch) flour tortillas

3½ cups (14 ounces) shredded Cheddar cheese

Sour cream, salsa and chopped green onion (optional)

1. Heat oil in large skillet over medium heat. Add onion; cook and stir 3 to 5 minutes or until tender. Add beef, salt, cumin, chili powder and garlic; cook and stir 6 to 8 minutes or until beef is browned. Drain fat. Stir in tomato sauce; cook until heated through. Stir in olives.

2. Make foil handles using three 18×2-inch strips of heavy-duty foil or use regular foil folded to double thickness. Crisscross foil in spoke design; place across bottom and up side of **CROCK-POT®** slow cooker. Lay 1 tortilla on foil strips. Spread with meat sauce and ½ cup cheese. Top with another tortilla, meat sauce and cheese. Repeat layers five times, ending with tortilla. Cover; cook on HIGH 1½ hours.

3. Lift out of **CROCK-POT®** slow cooker using foil handles; remove to large serving platter. Discard foil. Cut into wedges. Serve with sour cream, salsa and green onion, if desired.

SHREDDED BEEF FAJITAS

Makes 6 servings

1 beef flank steak (about 1 pound)

1 can (about 14 ounces) diced tomatoes with mild green chiles

1 cup chopped onion

½ medium green bell pepper, cut into ½-inch pieces

1 clove garlic, minced *or* ¼ teaspoon garlic powder

½ package (about 2 tablespoons) fajita seasoning mix

6 (8-inch) flour tortillas

Optional toppings: chopped fresh cilantro, guacamole, shredded Cheddar cheese and/or salsa

1. Cut beef into six portions; place in **CROCK-POT®** slow cooker. Combine tomatoes, onion, bell pepper, garlic and fajita seasoning mix in medium bowl; stir to blend. Pour over beef. Cover; cook on LOW 8 to 10 hours or on HIGH 4 to 5 hours.

2. Remove beef to large cutting board; shred with two forks. Stir beef back into **CROCK-POT®** slow cooker. To serve fajitas, place meat mixture evenly into tortillas. Top as desired; fold tortillas over meat mixture.

BEEF CHILE SAUCE

Makes 6 servings

2 tablespoons vegetable oil

2 pounds boneless beef round roast, cut into 1-inch pieces

1 medium yellow onion, finely chopped

2 cloves garlic, minced

1¾ cups water

5 canned whole mild green chiles, peeled and diced*

1 canned chipotle pepper in adobo sauce, diced

1 teaspoon salt

1 teaspoon all-purpose flour

1 teaspoon dried oregano

½ teaspoon ground cumin

¼ teaspoon black pepper

Prepared polenta (optional)

Sprigs fresh cilantro (optional)

Green chiles and chipotle peppers can sting and irritate the skin, so wear rubber gloves when handling peppers and do not touch your eyes.

1. Heat oil in large skillet over medium heat. Add beef; cook 6 to 8 minutes or until browned on all sides. Add onion and garlic during last few minutes of browning. Remove to **CROCK-POT®** slow cooker.

2. Add water, chiles and chipotle pepper; stir to combine. Cover; cook on LOW 2 hours.

3. Combine salt, flour, oregano, cumin and black pepper in small bowl; stir to blend. Add to **CROCK-POT®** slow cooker. Cover; cook on LOW 3 to 4 hours. Serve beef mixture over polenta, if desired. Garnish with cilantro.

SWEET AND SPICY PORK PICADILLO

Makes 4 servings

1 tablespoon olive oil

1 yellow onion, cut into ¼-inch pieces

2 cloves garlic, minced

1 pound boneless pork country-style ribs, trimmed and cut into 1-inch cubes

1 can (about 14 ounces) diced tomatoes

3 tablespoons cider vinegar

2 canned chipotle peppers in adobo sauce, chopped*

½ cup raisins

½ teaspoon ground cumin

½ teaspoon ground cinnamon

Hot cooked rice (optional)

Black beans (optional)

*You may substitute dried chipotle peppers, soaked in warm water about 20 minutes to soften before chopping.

1. Heat oil in large skillet over medium heat. Add onion and garlic; cook and stir 4 minutes. Add pork; cook and stir 5 to 7 minutes or until browned. Remove to **CROCK-POT®** slow cooker.

2. Combine tomatoes, vinegar, chipotle peppers, raisins, cumin and cinnamon in medium bowl; stir to blend. Pour over pork in **CROCK-POT®** slow cooker. Cover; cook on LOW 5 hours or on HIGH 3 hours. Remove pork to large cutting board; shred with two forks. Serve with rice and beans, if desired.

PORK TACOS WITH FRESH SALSA

Makes 10 servings

¼ cup all-purpose flour

1 teaspoon salt, divided

½ teaspoon black pepper, divided

1 pound pork shoulder roast, cubed

1 tablespoon vegetable oil

2 cloves garlic, minced

1 cup chicken broth

1 large red bell pepper, sliced into strips

1 medium zucchini, sliced then cut into fourths

1 large onion, sliced

3 medium plum tomatoes, seeded and chopped

2 tablespoons chopped onion

1 small jalapeño pepper, seeded and minced*

1 tablespoon chopped fresh cilantro

1 tablespoon lime juice

10 flour tortillas, warmed

*Jalapeño peppers can sting and irritate the skin, so wear rubber gloves when handling peppers and do not touch your eyes.

1. Combine ¼ cup flour, ½ teaspoon salt and ¼ teaspoon pepper in large bowl; stir to blend. Add pork; toss to coat. Heat oil in large skillet over medium-high heat. Add pork and garlic; cook and stir 6 to 8 minutes or until pork is browned on all sides. Remove pork mixture to **CROCK-POT®** slow cooker using slotted spoon.

2. Add broth to skillet, stirring to scrape up any browned bits. Pour broth mixture into **CROCK-POT®** slow cooker. Add bell pepper, zucchini and onion slices. Cover; cook on LOW 7 to 8 hours.

3. Meanwhile, combine, tomatoes, chopped onion, jalapeño pepper, cilantro, lime juice, ½ teaspoon salt and ¼ teaspoon pepper in small bowl. Refrigerate until ready to serve.

ANCHO CHILE AND LIME PORK TACOS

Makes 10 to 12 servings

2 large plantain leaves

1 boneless pork shoulder roast
(4 to 6 pounds) or pork chops*

Juice of 4 to 5 medium limes

1 package (about 1 ounce) ancho
chile paste

Salt

1 large onion, sliced

Pickled Red Onions (recipe follows)

Flour tortillas

Lime wedges (optional)

Cilantro-Lime Rice (optional)

*Unless you have a 5-, 6- or 7-quart CROCK-POT®
slow cooker, cut any roast larger than 2½ pounds
in half so it cooks completely.*

Line **CROCK-POT®** slow cooker with plantain leaves; top with pork roast. Combine lime juice, chile paste and salt in medium bowl until well blended. Add paste mixture and onion to **CROCK-POT®** slow cooker; wrap leaves over pork. Cover; cook on LOW 8 to 10 hours. Prepare Pickled Red Onions. Serve with tortillas. Top with Pickled Red Onions. Serve with Cilantro-Lime Rice, if desired.

PICKLED RED ONIONS: Combine 1 cup sliced red onion and juice from 1 to 2 limes in small bowl; set aside until juice is absorbed. Makes 1 cup.

CILANTRO-LIME RICE: Prepare rice according to package directions. Add 2 to 4 tablespoons butter, ¼ to ½ cup chopped fresh cilantro, juice of 2 to 4 medium limes and ½ to 1 teaspoon salt. Makes 10 to 12 servings.

CHORIZO BURRITOS

Makes 4 to 5 servings

15 ounces chorizo sausage, casings removed

1 can (about 15 ounces) red kidney beans, rinsed and drained

1 can (about 14 ounces) diced tomatoes

1 can (11 ounces) corn, drained

2 green or red bell peppers, cut into 1-inch pieces

1 cup chicken broth

½ teaspoon ground cumin

½ teaspoon ground cinnamon

8 to 10 flour tortillas, warmed

Hot cooked rice

Shredded Monterey Jack cheese or sour cream

1. Combine chorizo, beans, tomatoes, corn, bell peppers, broth, cumin and cinnamon in **CROCK-POT®** slow cooker; stir to blend. Cover; cook on LOW 6 to 8 hours.

2. Spoon filling down centers of warm tortillas; top with rice and shredded cheese. Roll up to serve.

ROUGH-CUT SMOKY RED PORK

Makes 8 servings

1 boneless pork shoulder roast (about 4 pounds)*

1 can (about 14 ounces) stewed tomatoes, drained

1 can (6 ounces) tomato paste with basil, oregano and garlic

1 cup chopped red bell pepper

2 to 3 canned chipotle peppers in adobo sauce, finely chopped and mashed with fork**

1 teaspoon salt

1½ to 2 tablespoons sugar

*Unless you have a 5-, 6- or 7-quart CROCK-POT® slow cooker, cut any roast larger than 2½ pounds in half so it cooks completely.

**For less heat, remove seeds from chipotle peppers before mashing.

1. Coat inside of **CROCK-POT®** slow cooker with nonstick cooking spray. Place pork, fat side up, in bottom. Combine tomatoes, tomato paste, bell pepper, chipotle peppers and salt in medium bowl; pour over pork.

2. Cover; cook on HIGH 5 hours. Scrape tomato mixture into cooking liquid. Remove pork to large cutting board; let stand 15 minutes. Stir sugar into cooking liquid. Cook, uncovered, on HIGH 15 minutes.

3. To serve, remove fat from pork and slice. Pour sauce over pork slices.

SPICY CITRUS PORK WITH PINEAPPLE SALSA

Makes 6 servings

1½ teaspoons ground cumin

½ teaspoon black pepper

¼ teaspoon salt

1½ pounds center-cut pork loin

1 tablespoon vegetable oil

2 cans (8 ounces *each*) pineapple tidbits in juice, drained and juice reserved*

2 tablespoons lemon juice, divided

½ cup finely chopped orange or red bell pepper

2 tablespoons finely chopped red onion

1 tablespoon chopped fresh cilantro or mint

1 teaspoon grated lemon peel

½ teaspoon grated fresh ginger

⅛ teaspoon red pepper flakes (optional)

If tidbits are unavailable, purchase pineapple chunks and coarsely chop.

1. Coat inside of **CROCK-POT®** slow cooker with nonstick cooking spray. Combine cumin, black pepper and salt in small bowl. Rub evenly onto pork. Heat oil in medium skillet over medium-high heat. Add pork; cook 6 to 8 minutes or until browned on all sides. Remove to **CROCK-POT®** slow cooker.

2. Spoon 2 tablespoons reserved pineapple juice and 1 tablespoon lemon juice over pork. Cover; cook on LOW 2 hours or on HIGH 1 hour or until meat thermometer registers 160°F and pork is barely pink in center.

3. Meanwhile, toss pineapple, remaining 2 tablespoons pineapple juice, remaining 1 tablespoon lemon juice, bell pepper, onion, cilantro, lemon peel, ginger and red pepper flakes, if desired, in medium bowl.

4. Remove pork to large cutting board. Cover loosely with foil; let stand 10 to 15 minutes before slicing. Pour juices evenly over pork. Serve with salsa.

PULLED PORK ENCHILADAS

Makes 6 servings

1 can (about 14 ounces) chicken broth

1 medium onion, chopped

2 minced canned chipotle peppers in adobo sauce, plus 1 tablespoon adobo sauce

2 cloves garlic, minced

2 teaspoons ground cumin

1 teaspoon ground cinnamon

1 teaspoon salt

½ teaspoon black pepper

1 boneless pork shoulder roast (5¾ pounds), trimmed*

1 can (19 ounces) enchilada sauce, divided

1 jar prepared salsa

1 cup (4 ounces) shredded Mexican cheese blend, divided

1 can (4 ounces) diced mild green chiles

12 (6-inch) flour tortillas

Sour cream (optional)

Sprigs fresh cilantro (optional)

*Unless you have a 5-, 6- or 7-quart CROCK-POT® slow cooker, cut any roast larger than 2½ pounds in half so it cooks completely.

1. Combine broth, onion, chipotle peppers, adobo sauce and garlic in **CROCK-POT®** slow cooker. Combine cumin, cinnamon, salt and black pepper in small bowl; rub onto top of pork. Place pork in **CROCK-POT®** slow cooker, seasoned side up. Cover; cook on LOW 12 to 14 hours or on HIGH 6 to 7 hours.

2. Remove pork to large cutting board; shred with two forks. Measure 3 cups; reserve remaining pork for another use.

3. Preheat oven to 375°F. Combine 3 cups pork, 1 cup enchilada sauce, salsa and ¾ cup cheese in large bowl. Spread ½ cup enchilada sauce and diced green chiles in 13×9-inch baking dish. Spread ¼ cup pork mixture on each tortilla. Roll up and place seam side down in baking dish. Spread remaining enchilada sauce over tortillas.

4. Bake 20 minutes. Top with remaining ¼ cup cheese; bake 5 minutes or until cheese is melted. Serve with sour cream and cilantro, if desired.

CHIPOTLE TACOS

Makes 8 servings

2 pounds ground beef

2 cans (about 15 ounces *each*) pinto beans, rinsed and drained

2 cups chopped onions

1 can (about 14 ounces) diced tomatoes with peppers and onions, drained

2 chipotle peppers in adobo sauce, mashed

1 tablespoon beef bouillon granules

1 tablespoon sugar

1½ teaspoons ground cumin

16 taco shells or flour tortillas

Shredded lettuce and shredded Cheddar cheese (optional)

1. Brown beef in large nonstick skillet over medium-high heat 6 to 8 minutes, stirring to break up meat. Drain fat.

2. Combine beef, beans, onions, tomatoes, chipotle peppers, bouillon granules, sugar and cumin in **CROCK-POT®** slow cooker. Cover; cook on LOW 4 hours or on HIGH 2 hours. Serve filling in taco shells. Top with lettuce and cheese, if desired.

VEGETARIAN FIESTA

BLACK BEAN, ZUCCHINI AND CORN ENCHILADAS

Makes 6 servings

1 tablespoon vegetable oil

1 medium onion, chopped

2 medium zucchini

2 cups corn

1 large red bell pepper, chopped

1 teaspoon minced garlic

½ teaspoon salt

½ teaspoon ground cumin

¼ teaspoon ground coriander

1 can (about 14 ounces) black beans, rinsed and drained

2 jars (16 ounces *each*) salsa verde

12 (6-inch) corn tortillas

2½ cups (10 ounces) shredded Monterey Jack cheese

2 tablespoons chopped fresh cilantro

1. Heat oil in large skillet over medium heat. Add onion; cook 6 minutes or until softened. Add zucchini, corn and bell pepper; cook 2 minutes. Add garlic, salt, cumin and coriander; cook and stir 1 minute. Stir in beans. Remove from heat.

2. Pour 1 cup salsa in bottom of **CROCK-POT®** slow cooker. Arrange 3 tortillas in single layer, cutting tortillas in half as needed to make them fit. Place 2 cups vegetable mixture over tortillas; sprinkle with ½ cup cheese. Repeat layering two more times. Layer with remaining 3 tortillas; top with 2 cups salsa. Sprinkle with remaining 1 cup cheese. Reserve remaining filling and salsa for another use.

3. Cover; cook on HIGH 2 hours or until cheese is bubbly and edges are lightly browned. Sprinkle with cilantro. Turn off heat. Let stand, uncovered, 10 minutes before serving.

BEAN RAGOÛT WITH CILANTRO-CORNMEAL DUMPLINGS

Makes 6 servings

2 cans (about 14 ounces *each*) diced tomatoes

1 can (about 15 ounces) pinto or kidney beans, rinsed and drained

1 can (about 15 ounces) black beans, rinsed and drained

1½ cups chopped red bell peppers

1 onion, chopped

2 zucchini, sliced

½ cup chopped green bell pepper

½ cup chopped celery

1 poblano pepper, seeded and chopped*

2 cloves garlic, minced

3 tablespoons chili powder

2 teaspoons ground cumin

1 teaspoon dried oregano

¼ teaspoon salt

⅛ teaspoon black pepper

Cilantro-Cornmeal Dumplings (recipe follows)

Poblano peppers can sting and irritate the skin, so wear rubber gloves when handling peppers and do not touch your eyes.

1. Combine tomatoes, beans, red bell peppers, onion, zucchini, green bell pepper, celery, poblano pepper, garlic, chili powder, cumin, oregano, salt and black pepper in **CROCK-POT®** slow cooker; stir to blend. Cover; cook on LOW 7 to 8 hours.

2. Prepare Cilantro-Cornmeal dumplings 1 hour before serving. Turn **CROCK-POT®** slow cooker to HIGH. Drop dumplings by level tablespoonfuls (larger dumplings will not cook properly) on top of ragoût. Cover; cook on HIGH 1 hour or until toothpick inserted into dumplings comes out clean.

CILANTRO-CORNMEAL DUMPLINGS

¼ cup all-purpose flour

¼ cup yellow cornmeal

½ teaspoon baking powder

¼ teaspoon salt

1 tablespoon shortening

1 tablespoon shredded Cheddar cheese

2 teaspoons minced fresh cilantro

¼ cup milk

Mix flour, cornmeal, baking powder and salt in medium bowl. Cut in shortening with pastry blender or two knives until mixture resembles coarse crumbs. Stir in cheese and cilantro. Pour milk into flour mixture; stir just until dry ingredients are moistened.

CHILE RELLEÑOS

Makes 6 servings

6 whole poblano peppers*

2½ cups (10 ounces) grated Chihuahua cheese or queso fresco, divided

½ cup plus 2 tablespoons prepared salsa verde, divided

¼ cup plus 2 tablespoons fresh cilantro, divided

1 (1-inch) piece fresh serrano pepper*

1 large clove garlic

1 can (12 ounces) evaporated milk

2 tablespoons all-purpose flour

2 eggs

⅔ cup sour cream

Poblano and serrano peppers can sting and irritate the skin, so wear rubber gloves when handling peppers and do not touch your eyes.

1. Coat inside of **CROCK-POT®** slow cooker with nonstick cooking spray. Place poblano peppers under broiler, about 4 inches from heat. Broil just until skins blister. Let cool slightly in large paper bag. Peel peppers. Cut down one side of each pepper; open flat to remove any seeds or membranes inside. Pat dry with paper towels.

2. Divide 1½ cups cheese evenly among peppers; roll to enclose. Lay peppers in single layer in bottom of **CROCK-POT®** slow cooker.

3. Combine ½ cup salsa verde, ¼ cup cilantro, serrano pepper and garlic in food processor or blender; pulse. Add milk, flour and eggs; process until smooth. Pour salsa mixture over poblano peppers; top with remaining 1 cup cheese. Cover; cook on LOW 3 hours.

4. Meanwhile, combine sour cream and remaining 2 tablespoons salsa verde in small bowl; stir to blend. Refrigerate sour cream mixture until ready to serve.

5. If desired, remove poblano peppers from **CROCK-POT®** slow cooker onto large baking sheet. Broil 3 to 5 minutes. Garnish with sour cream mixture and remaining 2 tablespoons cilantro.

LAYERED MEXICAN-STYLE CASSEROLE

Makes 6 servings

2 cans (about 15 ounces *each*) hominy, drained

1 can (about 15 ounces) black beans, rinsed and drained

1 can (about 14 ounces) diced tomatoes with garlic, basil and oregano

1 cup thick and chunky salsa

1 can (6 ounces) tomato paste

½ teaspoon ground cumin

3 (9-inch) flour tortillas

2 cups (8 ounces) shredded Monterey Jack cheese

¼ cup sliced black olives

1. Prepare foil handles by tearing off three 18×2-inch strips of heavy-duty foil or use regular foil folded to double thickness. Crisscross foil strips in spoke design and place in **CROCK-POT®** slow cooker.

2. Coat inside of **CROCK-POT®** slow cooker with nonstick cooking spray. Combine hominy, beans, tomatoes, salsa, tomato paste and cumin in large bowl; stir to blend.

3. Press 1 tortilla in bottom of **CROCK-POT®** slow cooker. Top with one third of hominy mixture and one third of cheese. Repeat layers. Press remaining tortilla on top. Top with remaining hominy mixture. Set aside remaining one third cheese.

4. Cover; cook on LOW 6 to 8 hours or on HIGH 2 to 3 hours. Turn off heat. Sprinkle with remaining cheese and olives. Cover; let stand 5 minutes. Pull out tortilla stack with foil handles. Cut into six wedges.

BEAN AND VEGETABLE BURRITOS

Makes 4 servings

2 tablespoons chili powder

2 teaspoons dried oregano

1½ teaspoons ground cumin

1 sweet potato, diced

1 can (about 15 ounces) black beans, rinsed and drained

4 cloves garlic, minced

1 onion, halved and thinly sliced

1 jalapeño pepper, seeded and minced*

1 green bell pepper, chopped

1 cup frozen corn, thawed and drained

3 tablespoons lime juice

1 tablespoon chopped fresh cilantro

½ cup (3 ounces) shredded Monterey Jack cheese

4 (10-inch) flour tortillas

Jalapeño peppers can sting and irritate the skin, so wear rubber gloves when handling peppers and do not touch your eyes.

1. Combine chili powder, oregano and cumin in small bowl.

2. Layer sweet potato, beans, half of chili powder mixture, garlic, onion, jalapeño pepper, bell pepper, remaining half of chili powder mixture and corn in **CROCK-POT®** slow cooker. Cover; cook on LOW 5 hours or until sweet potato is tender. Stir in lime juice and cilantro.

3. Preheat oven to 350°F. Spoon 2 tablespoons cheese down center of each tortilla. Top with 1 cup filling. Fold up bottom edges of tortillas over filling; fold in sides and roll to enclose filling. Place burritos seam side down on baking sheet. Cover with foil; bake 20 minutes or until heated through.

MEXICAN HOT POT

Makes 6 servings

1 tablespoon canola oil

1 medium onion, chopped

3 cloves garlic, minced

2 teaspoons red pepper flakes

2 teaspoons dried oregano

1 teaspoon ground cumin

1 can (28 ounces) whole tomatoes, drained and chopped

2 cups corn

1 can (about 15 ounces) chickpeas, rinsed and drained

1 can (about 15 ounces) pinto beans, rinsed and drained

1 cup water

1½ cups shredded iceberg lettuce

1. Heat oil in large skillet over medium-high heat. Add onion and garlic; cook and stir 5 minutes. Stir in red pepper flakes, oregano and cumin. Remove onion and garlic mixture to **CROCK-POT**® slow cooker using slotted spoon.

2. Stir in tomatoes, corn, chickpeas, pinto beans and water. Cover; cook on LOW 7 to 8 hours or on HIGH 2 to 3 hours. Top each serving with lettuce.

MEXICAN-STYLE RICE AND CHEESE

Makes 6 to 8 servings

1 can (about 15 ounces) Mexican-style beans

1 can (about 14 ounces) diced tomatoes with mild green chiles

2 cups (8 ounces) shredded Monterey Jack or Colby cheese, divided

1½ cups uncooked converted long grain rice

1 large onion, finely chopped

½ (4 ounces) package cream cheese

3 cloves garlic, minced

1. Coat inside of **CROCK-POT®** slow cooker with nonstick cooking spray. Combine beans, tomatoes, 1 cup Monterey Jack cheese, rice, onion, cream cheese and garlic in **CROCK-POT®** slow cooker; stir to blend.

2. Cover; cook on LOW 6 to 8 hours. Sprinkle with remaining 1 cup Monterey Jack cheese just before serving.

POBLANO CREAMED CORN

Makes 6 servings

4 whole poblano peppers

3 tablespoons olive oil

1 package (16 ounces) frozen corn

3 slices American cheese

4 ounces cream cheese

2 tablespoons butter

1½ tablespoons vegetable broth

1 tablespoon chopped jalapeño pepper (optional)*

Salt and black pepper

*Jalapeño peppers can sting and irritate the skin, so wear rubber gloves when handling peppers and do not touch your eyes.

1. Preheat oven to 350°F. Spray large baking sheet with nonstick cooking spray. Place poblano peppers on prepared baking sheet; brush with oil. Bake 20 minutes or until outer skins loosen. When cool enough to handle, remove outer skin from 1 poblano pepper and mince. Cut remaining 3 poblano peppers in half and reserve.

2. Combine corn, American cheese, minced poblano pepper, cream cheese, butter, broth, jalapeño pepper, if desired, salt and black pepper in **CROCK-POT®** slow cooker. Cover; cook on LOW 4 to 5 hours. To serve, spoon corn into reserved poblano pepper halves.

RED BEANS AND RICE

Makes 6 servings

2 cans (about 15 ounces *each*) red kidney beans

1 can (about 14 ounces) diced tomatoes

½ cup chopped celery

½ cup chopped green bell pepper

½ cup chopped green onions

2 cloves garlic, minced

1 to 2 teaspoons hot pepper sauce

1 teaspoon Worcestershire sauce

1 whole bay leaf

3 cups hot cooked rice

1. Combine beans, tomatoes, celery, bell pepper, green onions, garlic, hot pepper sauce, Worcestershire sauce and bay leaf in **CROCK-POT®** slow cooker; stir to blend. Cover; cook on LOW 4 to 6 hours.

2. Mash mixture slightly in **CROCK-POT®** slow cooker with potato masher until mixture thickens. Turn **CROCK-POT®** slow cooker to HIGH. Cover; cook on HIGH 30 minutes. Remove and discard bay leaf. Serve bean mixture over rice.

SALSA–STYLE
MAC AND CHEESE

Makes 6 servings

1 **package (8 ounces) elbow macaroni, uncooked**

1 **can (about 14 ounces) diced tomatoes with green peppers and onions**

1 **can (10 ounces) diced tomatoes with mild green chiles**

1½ **cups salsa**

3 **cups (about 12 ounces) shredded Mexican cheese blend, divided**

1. Coat inside of **CROCK-POT®** slow cooker with nonstick cooking spray. Combine macaroni, tomatoes, salsa and 2 cups cheese in **CROCK-POT®** slow cooker; stir to blend. Cover; cook on LOW 3 hours 45 minutes or until macaroni is tender.

2. Sprinkle remaining 1 cup cheese over contents of **CROCK-POT®** slow cooker. Cover; cook on LOW 15 minutes or until cheese is melted.

ZESTY CORN AND BEANS

Makes 6 servings

1 tablespoon olive oil

1 large onion, diced

1 or 2 jalapeño peppers, chopped*

1 clove garlic, minced

2 cans (about 15 ounces *each*) red kidney beans, rinsed and drained

1 package (16 ounces) frozen corn, thawed

1 can (about 14 ounces) diced tomatoes

1 green bell pepper, cut into 1-inch pieces

2 teaspoons chili powder

¾ teaspoon salt

½ teaspoon ground cumin

½ teaspoon black pepper

Sour cream or plain yogurt (optional)

Sliced black olives (optional)

Jalapeño peppers can sting and irritate the skin, so wear rubber gloves when handling peppers and do not touch your eyes.

1. Heat oil in medium skillet over medium heat. Add onion, jalapeño pepper and garlic; cook and stir 5 minutes. Remove to **CROCK-POT®** slow cooker.

2. Add beans, corn, tomatoes, bell pepper, chili powder, salt, cumin and black pepper to **CROCK-POT®** slow cooker; stir to blend. Cover; cook on LOW 7 to 8 hours or on HIGH 3 to 4 hours. Serve with sour cream and black olives, if desired.

SERVING SUGGESTION: For a party, spoon this colorful vegetarian dish into hollowed-out bell peppers or bread bowls.

ON THE SIDE

FRIJOLES BORRACHOS (DRUNKEN BEANS)

Makes 8 servings

6 slices bacon, chopped

1 medium yellow onion, chopped

1 tablespoon minced garlic

3 jalapeño peppers, seeded and finely diced*

1 tablespoon dried oregano

1 can (12 ounces) beer

6 cups water

1 pound dried pinto beans, rinsed and sorted

1 can (about 14 ounces) diced tomatoes

1 tablespoon kosher salt

¼ cup chopped fresh cilantro

Jalapeño peppers can sting and irritate the skin, so wear rubber gloves when handling peppers and do not touch your eyes.

1. Heat large skillet over medium-high heat. Add bacon; cook 5 minutes or until mostly browned and crisp. Remove to **CROCK-POT®** slow cooker using slotted spoon. Discard all but 3 tablespoons of drippings.

2. Heat same skillet over medium heat. Add onion; cook 6 minutes or until softened and lightly browned. Add garlic, jalapeño peppers and oregano; cook 30 seconds or until fragrant. Increase heat to medium-high. Add beer; bring to a simmer. Cook 2 minutes, stirring and scraping any brown bits from bottom of skillet. Remove mixture to **CROCK-POT®** slow cooker.

3. Add water, beans, tomatoes and salt to **CROCK-POT®** slow cooker. Cover; cook on LOW 7 hours or on HIGH 3 to 4 hours or until beans are tender. Mash beans slightly until broth is thickened and creamy. Top with cilantro.

CONFETTI BLACK BEANS

Makes 6 servings

1 cup dried black beans, rinsed and sorted

3 cups water

1½ teaspoons olive oil

1 medium onion, chopped

¼ cup chopped red bell pepper

¼ cup chopped yellow bell pepper

1 jalapeño pepper, finely chopped*

1 large tomato, chopped

½ teaspoon salt

⅛ teaspoon black pepper

2 cloves garlic, minced

1 can (about 14 ounces) chicken broth

1 whole bay leaf

Hot pepper sauce (optional)

*Jalapeño peppers can sting and irritate the skin, so wear rubber gloves when handling peppers and do not touch your eyes.

1. Place beans in large bowl and add enough cold water to cover by at least 2 inches. Soak 6 to 8 hours or overnight.** Drain beans; discard water.

2. Heat oil in large skillet over medium heat. Add onion, bell peppers and jalapeño pepper; cook and stir 5 minutes or until onion is tender. Add tomato, salt and black pepper; cook 5 minutes. Stir in garlic.

3. Place beans, broth and bay leaf in **CROCK-POT®** slow cooker. Add onion mixture. Cover; cook on LOW 7 to 8 hours or on HIGH 4½ to 5 hours. Remove and discard bay leaf. Serve with hot pepper sauce, if desired.

**To quick soak beans, place beans in large saucepan; cover with water. Bring to a boil over high heat. Boil 2 minutes. Remove from heat; let soak, covered, 1 hour.

CHEESE GRITS WITH CHILES AND BACON

Makes 4 servings

6 slices bacon

1 to 2 serrano or jalapeño peppers, minced*

1 large shallot or small onion, finely chopped

4 cups chicken broth

1 cup uncooked grits**

½ teaspoon salt

¼ teaspoon black pepper

1 cup (4 ounces) shredded Cheddar cheese

½ cup half-and-half

2 tablespoons finely chopped green onion

*Serrano peppers can sting and irritate the skin, so wear rubber gloves when handling peppers and do not touch your eyes.

**Use coarse, instant, yellow or stone-ground grits.

1. Heat medium skillet over medium heat. Add bacon; cook until crisp. Remove to paper towel-lined plate using slotted spoon. Crumble 2 strips and place in **CROCK-POT®** slow cooker. Crumble and refrigerate remaining bacon.

2. Drain all but 1 tablespoon bacon drippings from skillet. Add serrano pepper and shallot; cook and stir 2 minutes or until shallot is lightly browned. Remove to **CROCK-POT®** slow cooker. Stir broth, grits, salt and black pepper into **CROCK-POT®** slow cooker. Cover; cook on LOW 4 hours.

3. Stir in cheese and half-and-half. Sprinkle with green onion and reserved bacon.

HOT THREE-BEAN CASSEROLE

Makes 12 servings

2 tablespoons olive oil

1 cup coarsely chopped onion

1 cup chopped celery

2 cloves garlic, minced

2½ cups (10 ounces) frozen cut green beans

1 can (about 15 ounces) chickpeas, rinsed and drained

1 can (about 15 ounces) kidney beans, rinsed and drained

1 cup coarsely chopped tomato

1 cup water

1 can (about 8 ounces) tomato sauce

1 to 2 jalapeño peppers, minced*

1 tablespoon chili powder

2 teaspoons sugar

1½ teaspoons ground cumin

1 teaspoon salt

1 teaspoon dried oregano

¼ teaspoon black pepper

Sprigs fresh oregano (optional)

Jalapeño peppers can sting and irritate the skin, so wear rubber gloves when handling peppers and do not touch your eyes.

1. Heat oil in large skillet over medium heat. Add onion, celery and garlic; cook and stir 5 minutes or until tender.

2. Combine onion mixture, green beans, chickpeas, kidney beans, chopped tomato, water, tomato sauce, jalapeño pepper, chili powder, sugar, cumin, salt, dried oregano and black pepper in **CROCK-POT®** slow cooker. Cover; cook on LOW 6 to 8 hours. Garnish with fresh oregano.

ARROZ CON QUESO

Makes 8 to 10 servings

1 can (16 ounces) crushed tomatoes, undrained

1 can (about 15 ounces) black beans, rinsed and drained

1½ cups uncooked converted long grain rice

1 onion, chopped

1 cup cottage cheese

1 can (4 ounces) chopped mild green chiles

2 tablespoons vegetable oil

3 teaspoons minced garlic

2 cups (8 ounces) shredded Monterey Jack cheese, divided

Sliced jalapeño pepper (optional)

Combine tomatoes, beans, rice, onion, cottage cheese, chiles, oil, garlic and 1 cup cheese in **CROCK-POT®** slow cooker; stir to blend. Cover; cook on LOW 6 to 9 hours or until liquid is absorbed. Sprinkle with remaining 1 cup cheese before serving. Garnish with jalapeño pepper.

MEXICAN CORN BREAD PUDDING

Makes 8 servings

1 can (about 14¾ ounces) cream-style corn

¾ cup yellow cornmeal

1 can (4 ounces) diced mild green chiles

2 eggs

2 tablespoons sugar

2 tablespoons vegetable oil

2 teaspoons baking powder

¾ teaspoon salt

½ cup (2 ounces) shredded Cheddar cheese

1. Coat inside of 2-quart **CROCK-POT®** slow cooker with nonstick cooking spray. Combine corn, cornmeal, chiles, eggs, sugar, oil, baking powder and salt in medium bowl; stir to blend. Pour into **CROCK-POT®** slow cooker.

2. Cover; cook on LOW 2 to 2½ hours or until center is set. Turn off heat. Sprinkle cheese over top. Cover; let stand 5 minutes or until cheese is melted.

SPICY BEANS

Makes 8 to 10 servings

⅓ cup dried lentils, rinsed and sorted

1⅓ cups water

5 slices bacon

1 onion, chopped

1 can (about 15 ounces) pinto beans, rinsed and drained

1 can (about 15 ounces) red kidney beans, rinsed and drained

1 can (about 14 ounces) diced tomatoes

3 tablespoons ketchup

3 cloves garlic, minced

1 teaspoon chili powder

½ teaspoon ground cumin

¼ teaspoon red pepper flakes

1 whole bay leaf

1. Boil lentils in water in large saucepan 20 to 30 minutes; drain.

2. Heat in medium skillet over medium heat. Add bacon; cook until crisp. Remove to paper towel-lined plate using slotted spoon. Cool and crumble bacon. In same skillet, cook and stir onion in bacon drippings over medium heat 3 to 4 minutes or until softened.

3. Combine lentils, bacon, onion, beans, tomatoes, ketchup, garlic, chili powder, cumin, red pepper flakes and bay leaf in **CROCK-POT®** slow cooker; stir to blend. Cover; cook on LOW 5 to 6 hours or on HIGH 3 to 4 hours. Remove and discard bay leaf before serving.

CHORIZO AND CORN DRESSING

Makes 4 to 6 servings

½ **pound chorizo sausage, removed from casings**

1 **can (about 14 ounces) chicken broth**

1 **can (10¾ ounces) condensed cream of chicken soup, undiluted**

1 **box (6 ounces) corn bread stuffing mix**

1 **cup chopped onion**

1 **cup diced red bell pepper**

1 **cup chopped celery**

1 **cup frozen corn**

3 **eggs, lightly beaten**

1. Coat inside of **CROCK-POT®** slow cooker with nonstick cooking spray. Heat large skillet over medium-high heat. Add chorizo; cook 6 to 8 minutes or until browned, stirring to break up meat. Remove to **CROCK-POT®** slow cooker using slotted spoon.

2. Whisk broth and soup into drippings in skillet over low heat. Add stuffing mix, onion, bell pepper, celery, corn and eggs; stir until well blended. Remove stuffing mixture to **CROCK-POT®** slow cooker. Cover; cook on LOW 7 hours or on HIGH 3½ hours.

MEXICAN-STYLE SPINACH

Makes 6 servings

3 packages (10 ounces *each*) frozen chopped spinach

1 tablespoon canola oil

1 onion, chopped

1 clove garlic, minced

2 Anaheim peppers, roasted, peeled and minced*

3 fresh tomatillos, roasted, husks removed and chopped**

To roast peppers, heat large heavy skillet over medium-high heat. Add peppers; cook and turn until blackened all over. Place peppers in brown paper bag 2 to 5 minutes. Remove peppers from bag; scrape off charred skin. Cut off top and pull out core. Slice lengthwise; scrape off veins and any remaining seeds with a knife.

**To roast tomatillos, heat large heavy skillet over medium heat. Add tomatillos with papery husks; cook 10 minutes or until husks are brown and interior flesh is soft. Remove and discard husks when cool enough to handle.*

Place spinach in **CROCK-POT®** slow cooker. Heat oil in large skillet over medium heat. Add onion and garlic; cook and stir 5 minutes or until onion is tender. Add Anaheim peppers and tomatillos; cook 3 to 4 minutes. Remove onion mixture to **CROCK-POT®** slow cooker. Cover; cook on LOW 4 to 6 hours.

ESCALLOPED CORN

Makes 6 servings

2 tablespoons butter	½ teaspoon salt
½ cup chopped onion	½ teaspoon dried thyme
3 tablespoons all-purpose flour	¼ teaspoon black pepper
1 cup milk	⅛ teaspoon ground nutmeg
4 cups frozen corn, thawed and divided	Sprigs fresh thyme (optional)

1. Melt butter in small saucepan over medium heat. Add onion; cook and stir 5 minutes or until tender. Add flour; cook and stir 1 minute. Stir in milk; bring to a boil over high heat. Boil 1 minute or until thickened, stirring constantly.

2. Process 2 cups corn in food processor or blender until coarsely chopped. Combine milk mixture, chopped and whole corn, salt, dried thyme, pepper and nutmeg in **CROCK-POT®** slow cooker; stir to blend.

3. Cover; cook on LOW 3½ to 4 hours or until mixture is bubbly around edge. Garnish with fresh thyme.

VARIATION: Add ½ cup (2 ounces) shredded Cheddar cheese and 2 tablespoons grated Parmesan cheese before serving; stir until melted. Garnish with additional shredded Cheddar cheese.

DESSERTS AND DRINKS

CLASSIC MARGARITA

Makes 10 to 12 servings

2 **cups water**	**Lime wedges**
10 **limes, cut into quarters**	**Coarse salt**
4 **cups tequila**	**Ice**
2 **cups triple sec**	

1. Combine water and limes in **CROCK-POT®** slow cooker. Cover; cook on HIGH 2 hours.

2. Strain into large pitcher. Stir in tequila and triple sec. Cover; refrigerate until chilled.

3. To serve, rub rim of margarita glasses with lime wedges; dip in salt. Fill cocktail shaker with ice; add margarita mixture. Shake until blended; strain into glasses. Garnish with lime wedges.

FROZEN MARGARITA: Rub rim of margarita glasses with lime wedges; dip in salt. Combine margarita mixture and 2 cups ice in blender; blend until smooth. Pour into prepared glasses; garnish with lime wedges. Makes 2 servings.

FROZEN STRAWBERRY MARGARITA: Rub rim of margarita glasses with lime wedges; dip in salt. Combine margarita mixture, 1 cup frozen strawberries and 1 cup ice in blender; blend until smooth. Pour into prepared glasses; garnish with lime wedges and strawberries. Makes 2 servings.

TRIPLE CHOCOLATE FANTASY

Makes 36 pieces

2 pounds white almond bark, broken into pieces

1 bar (4 ounces) sweetened chocolate, broken into pieces*

1 package (12 ounces) semisweet chocolate chips

2 cups coarsely chopped pecans, toasted**

⅛ teaspoon ground red pepper

*Use your favorite high-quality chocolate candy bar.

**To toast pecans, spread in single layer in heavy skillet. Cook and stir over medium heat 1 to 2 minutes or until nuts are lightly browned.

1. Line mini muffin pan with paper baking cups. Place bark, sweetened chocolate and chocolate chips in **CROCK-POT®** slow cooker. Cover; cook on HIGH 1 hour. *Do not stir.*

2. Turn **CROCK-POT®** slow cooker to LOW. Cover; cook on LOW 1 hour, stirring every 15 minutes. Stir in pecans and ground red pepper.

3. Drop mixture by tablespoonfuls into prepared baking cups; cool completely. Store in tightly covered container.

VARIATIONS: Here are a few ideas for other imaginative items to add in along with or instead of the pecans: raisins, crushed peppermint candy, candy-coated baking bits, crushed toffee, peanuts or pistachio nuts, chopped gum drops, chopped dried fruit, candied cherries, chopped marshmallows or sweetened coconut.

FIVE-SPICE APPLE CRISP

Makes 4 servings

3 tablespoons unsalted butter, melted

6 Golden Delicious apples, peeled and cut into ½-inch-thick slices

2 teaspoons lemon juice

¼ cup packed brown sugar

¾ teaspoon Chinese five-spice powder or ½ teaspoon ground cinnamon and ¼ teaspoon ground allspice, plus additional for garnish

1 cup coarsely crushed Chinese-style almond cookies or almond biscotti

Sweetened whipped cream (optional)

1. Butter inside of 5-quart **CROCK-POT®** slow cooker with melted butter. Add apples and lemon juice; toss to combine. Sprinkle apples with brown sugar and ¾ teaspoon five-spice powder; toss again. Cover; cook on LOW 3½ hours.

2. Spoon into bowls. Sprinkle cookies over apples. Garnish with whipped cream and additional five-spice powder.

DULCE DE LECHE

Makes about 1½ cups

**1 can (14 ounces) sweetened
    condensed milk**

1. Pour milk into 9×5-inch loaf pan. Cover tightly with foil. Place loaf pan in **CROCK-POT®** slow cooker. Pour enough water to reach halfway up sides of loaf pan. Cover; cook on LOW 5 to 6 hours or until golden and thickened.

2. Coat inside of **CROCK-POT®** "No Dial" slow cooker with nonstick cooking spray. Fill with warm dip.

SERVING SUGGESTION: Try this Dulce de Leche as a fondue with bananas, apples, shortbread, chocolate wafers, pretzels and/or waffle cookies.

PINEAPPLE RICE PUDDING

Makes 8 servings

1 can (20 ounces) crushed pineapple in juice, undrained

1 can (13½ ounces) unsweetened coconut milk

1 can (12 ounces) evaporated milk

¾ cup uncooked Arborio rice

2 eggs, lightly beaten

¼ cup granulated sugar

¼ cup packed brown sugar

½ teaspoon ground cinnamon

¼ teaspoon salt

¼ teaspoon ground nutmeg

Toasted coconut and pineapple slices (optional)*

Pineapple slices (optional)

*To toast coconut, spread in single layer in small heavy-bottomed skillet. Cook and stir over medium heat 1 to 2 minutes or until lightly browned. Remove from skillet immediately.

1. Combine crushed pineapple with juice, coconut milk, evaporated milk, rice, eggs, granulated sugar, brown sugar, cinnamon, salt and nutmeg in **CROCK-POT®** slow cooker; stir to blend. Cover; cook on HIGH 3 to 4 hours or until thickened and rice is tender.

2. Stir to blend. Serve warm or chilled. Garnish with toasted coconut and pineapple slices.

MOCHA SUPREME

Makes 8 servings

2 quarts strong brewed coffee

½ cup instant hot chocolate beverage mix

1 whole cinnamon stick, broken in half

¼ teaspoon ground red pepper

1 cup whipping cream

1 tablespoon powdered sugar

1. Place coffee, hot chocolate mix and cinnamon stick halves in **CROCK-POT®** slow cooker; stir. Cover; cook on HIGH 2 to 2½ hours or until heated through. Remove and discard cinnamon stick halves. Stir in ground red pepper.

2. Beat cream in medium bowl with electric mixer on high speed until soft peaks form. Add powdered sugar; beat until stiff peaks form. Ladle mocha mixture into mugs. Top with whipped cream.

TIP: To whip cream more quickly, chill the beaters and bowl in the freezer for 15 minutes.

MEXICAN CHOCOLATE BREAD PUDDING

Makes 6 to 8 servings

1½ cups whipping cream

4 ounces unsweetened chocolate, coarsely chopped

½ cup currants

2 eggs, beaten

½ cup sugar

1 teaspoon vanilla

¾ teaspoon ground cinnamon, plus additional for garnish

½ teaspoon ground allspice

⅛ teaspoon salt

3 cups Hawaiian-style sweet bread, challah or rich egg bread, cut into ½-inch cubes

Whipped cream (optional)

1. Heat whipping cream in large saucepan. Add chocolate; stir until melted.

2. Combine currants, eggs, sugar, vanilla, ¾ teaspoon cinnamon, allspice and salt in medium bowl; stir to blend. Add currant mixture to chocolate mixture; stir well to combine. Pour into **CROCK-POT®** slow cooker.

3. Gently fold in bread cubes using plastic spatula. Cover; cook on HIGH 3 to 4 hours or until knife inserted near center comes out clean.

4. Serve warm or chilled. Top with whipped cream sprinkled with additional cinnamon, if desired.

INFUSED MINT MOJITO

Makes 10 to 12 servings

2 cups water

2 cups sugar

2 bunches fresh mint, stems removed, plus additional for garnish

¾ to 1 cup fresh-squeezed lime juice

1 bottle (750 ml) light rum

2 liters club soda

Lime slices (optional)

1. Combine water, sugar and 2 bunches mint in **CROCK-POT®** slow cooker; stir to blend. Cover; cook on HIGH 3½ hours.

2. Strain into large pitcher. Stir in lime juice and rum. Cover and refrigerate until cold.

3. To serve, fill tall glasses with ice. Pour ¾ cup mint syrup over ice; top off with club soda. Garnish with additional fresh mint and lime slices. Serve immediately.

PUMPKIN CUSTARD

Makes 6 servings

1 cup canned solid-pack pumpkin

½ cup packed brown sugar

2 eggs, beaten

½ teaspoon ground ginger

½ teaspoon grated lemon peel

½ teaspoon ground cinnamon, plus additional for garnish

1 can (12 ounces) evaporated milk

1. Combine pumpkin, brown sugar, eggs, ginger, lemon peel and ½ teaspoon cinnamon in large bowl. Stir in evaporated milk. Divide mixture among six ramekins or custard cups. Cover each cup tightly with foil.

2. Place ramekins in **CROCK-POT®** slow cooker. Pour water into **CROCK-POT®** slow cooker to come about ½ inch from top of ramekins. Cover; cook on LOW 4 hours.

3. Use tongs or slotted spoon to remove ramekins from **CROCK-POT®** slow cooker. Sprinkle with additional ground cinnamon. Serve warm.

VARIATION: To make Pumpkin Custard in a single dish, pour custard into 1½-quart soufflé dish instead of ramekins. Cover with foil; place in **CROCK-POT®** slow cooker. (Place soufflé dish on two or three 18×2-inch strips of foil in **CROCK-POT®** slow cooker to make removal easier, if desired.) Add water to come 1½ inches from top of the soufflé dish. Cover; cook as directed above.

CHERRY FLAN

Makes 6 servings

5 eggs

½ cup sugar

½ teaspoon salt

¾ cup all-purpose flour

1 can (12 ounces) evaporated milk

1 teaspoon vanilla

1 bag (16 ounces) frozen, pitted dark sweet cherries, thawed

Sweetened whipped cream or cherry vanilla ice cream

1. Coat inside of **CROCK-POT®** slow cooker with nonstick cooking spray.

2. Beat eggs, sugar and salt in large bowl of electric mixer at high speed until thick and pale yellow. Add flour; beat until smooth. Beat in evaporated milk and vanilla.

3. Pour batter into **CROCK-POT®** slow cooker. Place cherries evenly over batter. Cover; cook on LOW 3½ to 4 hours or until flan is set. Serve warm with whipped cream.

SERVING SUGGESTION: Serve this dessert warm and top it with whipped cream or ice cream. Garnish with cherries and mint leaves for a special touch.

TEQUILA-POACHED PEARS

Makes 4 servings

4 Anjou pears, peeled
1 cup tequila
¾ cup sugar

Juice and peel of 1 lime, plus additional for garnish
1 can (11½ ounces) pear nectar
2 cups water

1. Place pears in **CROCK-POT®** slow cooker.

2. Add tequila, sugar, lime juice, lime peel, pear nectar and water to medium saucepan. Stir over medium-high heat until mixture boils. Boil 1 minute; pour over pears. Cover; cook on LOW 4 to 6 hours or on HIGH 2 to 3 hours or until pears are tender.

3. Serve on chilled plate drizzled with poaching liquid and sprinkled with additional lime peel.

TIP: Poaching fruit in a sugar, wine, juice or alcohol syrup helps the fruit retain its shape and adds flavor.

INDEX

METRIC CONVERSION CHART

VOLUME MEASUREMENTS (dry)

⅛ teaspoon = 0.5 mL
¼ teaspoon = 1 mL
½ teaspoon = 2 mL
¾ teaspoon = 4 mL
1 teaspoon = 5 mL
1 tablespoon = 15 mL
2 tablespoons = 30 mL
¼ cup = 60 mL
⅓ cup = 75 mL
½ cup = 125 mL
⅔ cup = 150 mL
¾ cup = 175 mL
1 cup = 250 mL
2 cups = 1 pint = 500 mL
3 cups = 750 mL
4 cups = 1 quart = 1 L

VOLUME MEASUREMENTS (fluid)

1 fluid ounce (2 tablespoons) = 30 mL
4 fluid ounces (½ cup) = 125 mL
8 fluid ounces (1 cup) = 250 mL
12 fluid ounces (1½ cups) = 375 mL
16 fluid ounces (2 cups) = 500 mL

WEIGHTS (mass)

½ ounce = 15 g
1 ounce = 30 g
3 ounces = 90 g
4 ounces = 120 g
8 ounces = 225 g
10 ounces = 285 g
12 ounces = 360 g
16 ounces = 1 pound = 450 g

DIMENSIONS

1/16 inch = 2 mm
⅛ inch = 3 mm
¼ inch = 6 mm
½ inch = 1.5 cm
¾ inch = 2 cm
1 inch = 2.5 cm

OVEN TEMPERATURES

250°F = 120°C
275°F = 140°C
300°F = 150°C
325°F = 160°C
350°F = 180°C
375°F = 190°C
400°F = 200°C
425°F = 220°C
450°F = 230°C

BAKING PAN SIZES

Utensil	Size in Inches/Quarts	Metric Volume	Size in Centimeters
Baking or Cake Pan (square or rectangular)	8×8×2	2 L	20×20×5
	9×9×2	2.5 L	23×23×5
	12×8×2	3 L	30×20×5
	13×9×2	3.5 L	33×23×5
Loaf Pan	8×4×3	1.5 L	20×10×7
	9×5×3	2 L	23×13×7
Round Layer Cake Pan	8×1½	1.2 L	20×4
	9×1½	1.5 L	23×4
Pie Plate	8×1¼	750 mL	20×3
	9×1¼	1 L	23×3
Baking Dish or Casserole	1 quart	1 L	—
	1½ quart	1.5 L	—
	2 quart	2 L	—